21-99   12/76

The ROYAL BRIDES

Leslie Frewin of London

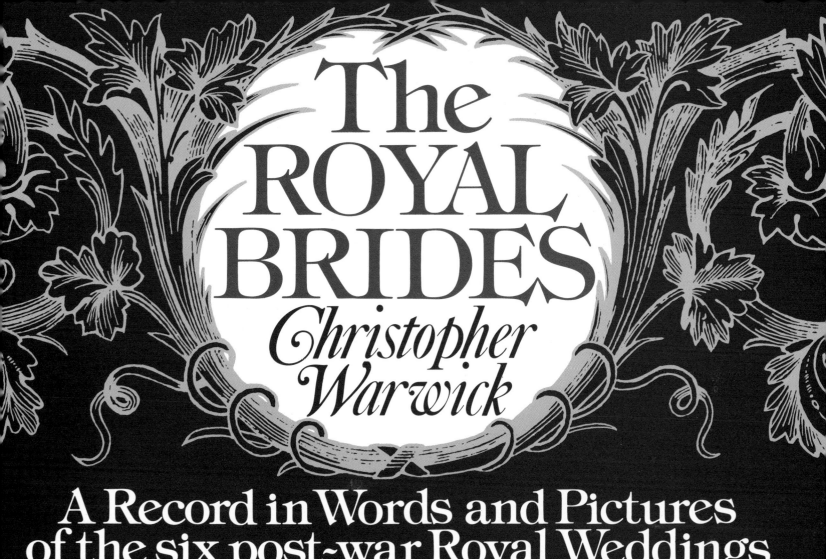

The ROYAL BRIDES

Christopher Warwick

A Record in Words and Pictures of the six post-war Royal Weddings

First published 1975 by
Leslie Frewin Publishers Limited,
Five Goodwin's Court,
Saint Martin's Lane,
London WC2N 4LL, England.

This book is set in 11 point on 13 Latinesque
Photoset, printed and bound in Great Britain by Weatherby
Woolnough, Sanders Road, Wellingborough, Northants.

ISBN 0 85632 143 5

FOR TWO VERY SPECIAL PEOPLE,
MY PARENTS, JOAN AND JOHN COLLINGS

CONTENTS

~INTRODUCTION~

Weddings, for most people, are essentially family occasions. But there are those whose marriages are of such importance that a truly quiet family service is an impossibility. This has been true through the ages particularly of the world's Royal Families.

Until relatively recent times, marriages in royal circles were generally made across politicians' tables. Politicians were all too aware that the marriage of two neighbouring royal heads would unite the respective countries and thereby cement a friendship useful in times both of war and peace. All too often royal parents promised their infant children to one another, with the consequence that the children were often desperately unhappy in marriage.

Mary, Queen of Scots became the bride of the Dauphin of France (later King Francis II) at the age of 15. Their wedding was as grandiose as any 16th century royal wedding, and indeed it was solemnized in one of the most beautiful buildings in the world, the Cathedral of Notre Dame in Paris.

Thrice married, Mary seemed unlucky in love. Two years after her marriage to the weakling king, she was widowed. Eventually she returned to Great Britain to take up her rightful place as Queen of Scotland. Mary's infatuation for Robert, Lord Darnley, despatched to Scotland by Elizabeth I, led them to the altar, and they were to become the parents of King James I of England and VI of Scotland. Ironically enough, he was to unite the two kingdoms of Scotland and England, long after his mother's head had fallen at Fotheringey Castle, and following the death of Elizabeth, Mary's cousin and political rival.

The Scottish queen's third marriage, to Lord Bothwell, had, like her marriage to Darnley, been motivated by the Queen of England. But though Mary's marriages were instigated by Elizabeth, it is generally assumed that she married for love.

Royal Houses still tend to become linked, as in the following instances, though it would seem ludicrous even to suppose that there might now be some political motivation behind the matches.

In 1960, King Baudoin of the Belgians was married to Dona Fabiola de Mora y Aragon of Spain, who could trace her ancestry back to Queen Catherine of Aragon, first wife of Henry VIII and widow of Henry's elder brother, Arthur; Princess Sophia of the Hellenes married Don Juan Carlos of Spain, now king-designate of that country, in Athens on 14th May 1962; on 18th September 1964 King Constantine of the Hellenes was married to Princess Anne-Marie of Denmark, again in Athens; and on 10th June 1967 the present Queen of Denmark, Margrethe, was married in Copenhagen to Count Henri da Laborde de Monpezat of France, now Prince Heinrich of Denmark.

The marriages of the British Royal Family are regulated by the Royal Marriages Act of 1772. The following extracts from the Act are taken from Halsbury's *Statutes of England*.

(1) No descendant of his late Majesty George II (other than the issue of princesses married, or who may marry into foreign families) shall be capable of contracting matrimony without the previous consent of His Majesty, his Heirs and successors etc., signified under the Great Seal, declared in Council and entered in the Privy Council books. Marriages of any such descendant without such consent to be void.

(2) Any such descendant, above twenty-five years old shall persist to contract a marriage without such consent, such descendant, after twelve months' notice to the Privy Council, may contract such marriage, which shall be good, unless both Houses of Parliament shall disapprove.

Thus, the Royal Marriages Act lays down the conditions under which members of the Royal Family can contract a valid marriage, and it is intended to guard against undesirable marriages which might affect the succession to the Throne.

The Royal Marriages Act did not apply, however, to the late Duke of Windsor since, in his abdication speech of 1936, the former king renounced not only his own rights to the Throne of England, but also the rights of any descendants. As is well known, the Duke and Duchess of Windsor did not have any children.

Nowadays, it is accepted that royal personages will marry for love; and it is now a well known fact that 'commoners' marry into the British Royal Family, as happened in recent years in the instances of the Princesses Anne, Margaret and Alexandra, the Duke of Kent and Prince Richard of Gloucester.

But despite the new informality, only one Royal wedding of recent times has passed off without any of the fuss or trappings of state. The occasion was the marriage of Prince Richard of Gloucester to the Danish Miss Birgitte Eva Van Deurs. Prince Richard was extremely fortunate in being able to have his wish for a quiet wedding fulfilled. Those nearer the Throne, or those even more in the public eye, are not so lucky. Public interest is naturally

aroused, and some of the trappings of State must go hand in hand with such ceremonies. Queen Victoria's children had a variety of weddings, ranging in venue from St Petersburg in Russia to a drawing room at Osborne House on the Isle of Wight and the picturesque church at Whippingham, also on the island. Twentieth century Royal weddings have all been much more public, entailing carriage processions, crowds, processional routes lined by the armed forces, bunting and the like. Royal weddings that have taken place in Britain this century have included the following:
February 1904, when Princess Alice of Albany, granddaughter of Queen Victoria, was married to the Earl of Athlone (the former Prince Alexander of Teck, brother of Queen Mary) at St George's Chapel, Windsor Castle; February 1919, when Princess Patricia of Connaught, also a granddaughter of Queen Victoria and daughter of the Duke of Connaught, married Captain Alexander Ramsay at Westminster Abbey; February 1922 saw the marriage of Princess Mary, daughter of King George V and Queen Mary, to Viscount Lascelles at Westminster Abbey; 26th April 1923, when the Duke of York, later King George VI, married the Lady Elizabeth Bowes-Lyon at Westminster; on 29th November 1934, the marriage of Prince George, Duke of Kent, to Princess Marina of Greece and Denmark was celebrated at Westminster Abbey and was followed by a Greek Orthodox service at Buckingham Palace; on 6th November 1935, Prince Henry, Duke of Gloucester, married the Lady Alice Montague-Douglas-Scott. The couple were to have been married at the Abbey, but due to the death of the bride's father, the Duke of Buccleuch, the service was conducted at the chapel of Buckingham Palace. On 20th November 1947, the first of the six post-War Royal weddings was that of the Princess Elizabeth to the Duke of Edinburgh at Westminster Abbey; on 6th May 1960 the Princess Margaret, younger daughter of King George VI and Queen Elizabeth, was married to Antony Armstrong-Jones at Westminster; 8th June 1961 saw the Duke of Kent marry Miss Katharine Worsley at York Minster; on 24th April 1963 Princess Alexandra of Kent was married to the Hon Angus Ogilvy at Westminster; on 8th July 1972 Prince Richard of Gloucester was married at St Andrews Church, Barnwell, Northamptonshire to Miss Birgitte Van Deurs; and on 14th November 1973, Princess Anne, the only daughter of Queen Elizabeth II and Prince Philip, Duke of Edinburgh, married Captain Mark Philips at Westminster Abbey.

Before the wedding of Prince Richard of Gloucester, there had been four princesses in the British Royal Family – Anne, Margaret, Alexandra and Alice, Countess of Athlone. In the foreseeable future we may expect to see only four more, attained, like the bride of Prince Richard, through marriage. At present the two most eligible bachelor princes are Charles, Prince of Wales, and his mother's cousin, Prince Michael of Kent. The two future royal bridegrooms who spring readily to mind are the Prince of Wales's younger brothers, Andrew and Edward. It would seem feasible, however, that when the latter princes attain their majority they may be created royal dukes, since there are several titles such as York and Connaught that have not been in use for many years. Should this occur, the line of royal duchesses, somewhat depleted, would be strengthened.

The British Royal Family can be looked upon as consisting of three distinct family units. The first is the family of the Queen and the Duke of Edinburgh with their four children, Charles, Andrew, Edward and Anne, and her husband Mark Phillips; The Queen's mother, Queen Elizabeth; and Her Majesty's sister, Princess Margaret with her husband, the Earl of Snowdon and their two children, David and Sarah.

The second family are the Gloucesters, consisting of The Dowager Duchess of Gloucester (now known as Princess Alice, Duchess of Gloucester), her son Richard and his wife Birgitte, now the Duke and Duchess of Gloucester, and their infant son, the Earl of Ulster.

The third unit is collectively known as the Kents. It consists of The Duke and Duchess of Kent with their three children, George, Nicholas and Helen; the Duke's sister, Princess Alexandra with her husband the Hon Angus Ogilvy and their two children James and Marina; and the Duke's younger brother, Prince Michael.

London, 1975   CW

~ELIZABETH AND PHILIP~

One can be forgiven for thinking that the British Royal Family is the most famous in the world – it is surely the most widely reported. The marriages of Royal ladies have always been the subject of speculation and in 1946 the Belgian newspapers ran articles implying the marriage of 41-year-old Prince Charles of Belgium to 'an English Princess'. The Heiress Presumptive? In the United States however, the press had already begun to nose out the romance between the 20-year-old Elizabeth and the 26-year-old Prince Philip of Greece.

Almost three decades have passed since Princess Elizabeth Alexandra Mary, elder daughter of King George VI and Queen Elizabeth, was married to a man she first met as a child of thirteen.

The tall naval officer was born a prince of the Royal House of Greece and Denmark on 10th June 1921, the only son and youngest of five children of Prince and Princess Andrew of Greece. Philip's birthplace was an unpretentious house on the island of Corfu known as Mon Repos.

The history of the Greek Royal House is punctuated by trouble, military coups and exile, and the young prince was little used to the grandeur of royal palaces. When he was still a child, his family left Greece to live in quiet exile at St Cloud near Paris. Here he received his first lessons before coming to England where he attended Tabor's Preparatory School at Cheam. He was subsequently to attend Gordonstoun, followed by the Royal Naval College at Dartmouth, where as the best all round cadet he earned the King's Dirk and the Eardley-Howard-Crocket prize. In the Royal Navy he was listed as 'Prince Philip', but known to all merely as Philip.

His mother, Princess Alice, was a sister of Earl Mountbatten of Burma. His maternal grandmother was Princess Victoria of Battenberg, his great-grandmother, Princess Alice of Hesse; and both he and Princess Elizabeth shared in common the same great-great-grandmother, Queen Victoria.

With the threat of World War II, King George VI had expressed a wish to see how naval training was progressing, and on 22nd July 1939 His Majesty, accompanied by the Queen, the two Princesses and Lord Mountbatten, sailed for Dartmouth aboard the old Royal Yacht, the *Victoria and Albert*.

An epidemic of chicken-pox had broken out, and because of the risk of infection the Princesses remained at the Captain's house instead of attending morning chapel with their parents. There, set

the task of keeping the two girls amused, was Prince Philip, then an eighteen-year-old cadet, who was feeling rather nonplussed at the duty to which he had been detailed.

As Princess Elizabeth grew older, she and the prince were inevitably to see more of each other, and indeed a photograph of her distant cousin occupied a place in her room.

Having kept their ensuing romance as quiet as was humanly possible, the betrothal of the Princess to Prince Philip was announced by the King and Queen on 10th July 1947, following the Royal Family's return from an extensive tour of South Africa, where Princess Elizabeth with her sister Margaret took the opportunity on their early morning rides to find a deserted telephone from where Elizabeth was able to make calls to Philip in London.

On the morning of 10th July, Princess Elizabeth and her fiancé posed for the first official engagement photographs on the terraces and lawns of Buckingham Palace, the Princess wearing her diamond engagement ring. Following the photographs, Princess Elizabeth accompanied her parents to Westminster Abbey for a service dedicating the Battle of Britain chapel.

Five months before the couple's engagement was announced, Philip had formally relinquished his royal style and titles together with his Greek nationality, and had become a naturalised British subject. At the same time he adopted the name of Mountbatten which was the anglicised name adopted by his mother's family in 1917 when, owing to the War with Germany, King George V had declared that all Germanic connections were to be severed.

Princess Elizabeth and Lieutenant Philip Mountbatten, it was announced, would be married on the morning of 20th November 1947 at Westminster Abbey. It was the first wedding in the Royal Family since that of the Duke and Duchess of Gloucester at Buckingham Palace twelve years before in November 1935.

The war had ended two years before but an air of austerity still prevailed, with the result that clothing coupons were still in existence. Like other British families, the Royal Family were included in the number of recipients, and the bride-to-be was obliged to save her coupons for the gown she would wear. The dress itself was to be designed by Mr Norman Hartnell, who was to become dressmaker to the Queen and several of the royal ladies. He had, ten years before, been responsible for the design of the gowns worn by the Maids-of-Honour in attendance on

Queen Elizabeth, when she and King George VI were crowned at Westminster Abbey in May 1937.

Hartnell's first venture into the world of society weddings came when he was commissioned to make the wedding gown for the bride of the Marquess of Bath, and at that time it was described as 'the Eighth Wonder of the World'. His first royal wedding dress was that worn by the Dowager Duchess of Gloucester (Princess Alice, Duchess of Gloucester) at her marriage in 1935 to the late Duke. Because of the death of her father shortly before, the bride wore a gown in the palest shell pink satin, with a matching full length veil.

He was subsequently responsible for an entire range of successful outfits for members of the Royal Family, and in 1957 when Princess Elizabeth, by now Queen, paid a State Visit to Paris, he was acclaimed by the whole world for the ball gowns he designed for her. Dior himself referred to Hartnell as 'The Master'.

Those present at the Royal Wedding included: King Frederick IX and Queen Ingrid of Denmark; King Peter and Queen Alexandra of Yugoslavia; King Michael of Rumania: King Haakon of Norway, with his son, Crown Prince Olav; Queen Frederika of the Hellenes; The Princess Regent of the Netherlands (Crown Princess Juliana) and Prince Bernhard of the Netherlands; Crown Prince Gustav Adolf of Sweden, with Crown Princess Louise; Queen Victoria-Eugenie of Spain; the Duchess of Aosta; Princess Eugenie of the Hellenes; Princess Elizabeth and Prince John of Luxembourg; and Prince and Princess Rene de Bourbon-Parme.

Princess Elizabeth's attendants were to be ten in number, eight bridesmaids and two page-boys. The bridesmaids were: The Princess Margaret, Princess Alexandra of Kent, Lady Mary Cambridge (a great-niece of Queen Mary), Lady Caroline Montague-Douglas-Scott, Lady Pamela Mountbatten (younger daughter of Earl and Countess Mountbatten of Burma), Lady Elizabeth Lambart, the Hon Margaret Elphinstone and Miss Diana Bowes-Lyon. The two page boys were Prince William of Gloucester and his cousin, Prince Michael of Kent. The bridegroom had asked the Marquess of Milford Haven to act as Groomsman.

The nation was delighted at the prospect of the wedding—the first colourful royal occasion since the end of the War. The numbers who flocked to London were in their tens of thousands. They came, as always, to catch the best glimpse possible of Britain's future Queen and the newly created Duke of Edinburgh. (On 19th November, the day before the wedding, King George VI had created Lieutenant Mountbatten His Royal Highness, The Duke of Edinburgh.)

The day of the wedding was a typical winter's day—damp and cold, with overcast skies. But still the crowds were not to be daunted, filling the streets of the processional route to bursting point. Trafalgar Square was a solid mass of humanity, stretching up to the steps of the Church of St Martins-in-the-Fields, and almost the whole way up Northumberland Avenue, a street barely to be touched upon by the wedding party. Seats specially erected for the wedding were being sold for up to £150 each.

Queen Elizabeth drove to Westminster Abbey in the Glass Coach, accompanied by Princess Margaret who was to act as the chief bridesmaid. The Queen was wearing a long gown of apricot and gold, with her blue sash of the Order of the Garter. Queen Mary, the much revered Queen Mother, wore a dress of silver and deep midnight blue, and the only member of the Royal Family not present was the bride's aunt, the Princess Royal, who was unwell.

Shortly before the arrival of the bride, and following the visiting royal heads and privileged guests, the bridal attendants arrived at the West Door and stood together awaiting Princess Elizabeth and the King.

The two small page-boys wore kilts of Royal Stuart Tartan and white silk shirts, and the eight bridesmaids wore dresses inspired by paintings hung in Buckingham Palace by the Victorian artists, Winterhalter, Tuxen and Sir George Hayter. The diaphanous skirts of white silk tulle, mounted with stars, floral sprays and orange blossom, were to complement the gown worn by Princess Elizabeth, and their spray head-dresses resembled the bands of laurel leaves worn by Roman emperors.

Finally, to the cheers of the crowds and a fanfare of trumpets, the bride arrived on the arm of His Majesty King George VI, immaculate in naval uniform.

For her gown, Princess Elizabeth had chosen a classic style, made from heavy ivory duchess satin. The fabric had been made in Dunfermline by the Scottish firm of Winterthur, and designs of stars and ears of corn were worked on it with 10,000 seed pearls. Inspired by a Botticelli painting, the gown was complemented by a full shoulder train of white silk tulle, again worked with designs of the roses of York, star flowers and orange blossom in pearl and crystal. The long veil, also of silk tulle, fell from a diamond tiara, loaned by her mother. (It was also loaned to Princess Anne for her wedding in 1973.) The tiara had caused a jeweller to go scurrying to Buckingham Palace shortly before the bride was due to leave for the Abbey, as the band had snapped. In her hands Princess Elizabeth carried a bouquet of orchids. That too had caused a panic at the palace, when at first it could not be found. Eventually it was located in a refrigerator, where a footman had placed it to keep the blooms fresh.

The King had driven with his daughter beside him to the Abbey in the Irish State Coach, complete with a Sovereign's Escort of the Household Cavalry. They rode between the lines of troops lining the processional route, behind whom were packed the thousands who cheered them on their way. Eight members of the ATS were also selected to join the Princess's Guard-of-Honour as she had been a member during the War. Inside the Abbey, the King led his daughter solemnly along the aisle and under the ornate organ screen to the steps of the High Altar, where the Duke of Edinburgh awaited them.

The Archbishops of Canterbury and York, and the Dean of Westminster, Canon Don, officiated at the service, and the King stood silently beside his daughter as she became Her Royal Highness The Princess Elizabeth, Duchess of Edinburgh. The two page-boys stood completely still, holding the bridal train, and behind them was Princess Margaret, holding her sister's bouquet.

The form of Service was taken from the form of marriage used in every Church of England ceremony, and at the conclusion of the service, following the Benediction and Anthem, the great fanfare of the Master of the King's Musik rang out from the Kneller Hall Trumpets, and Mendelssohn's Wedding March was played. This celebrated composition had been given its inaugural performance at an earlier royal wedding, that of Vicky (The Princess Royal), eldest daughter of Queen Victoria, in January 1858 when she married the son of the Kaiser, Prince Frederick William of Prussia. The bride curtsied to their Majesties and the bridegroom bowed. The procession reformed and the Princess and her husband made their way back along the central aisle, followed by their attendants.

The carriage processions rolled back in state to Buckingham Palace for the wedding breakfast, during which Princess Elizabeth and her husband cut the wedding cake with the Duke's ceremonial sword. The sword had belonged to Philip's grandfather, Prince Louis of Battenberg, First Marquess of Milford Haven. The wedding cake stood nine feet high, in four tiers, weighed 500 pounds, and was embellished with musical cupids under canopies bearing the respective coats-of-arms of the bridal couple. A wedge of cake on the lower tier had already been cut and bound with satin ribbon so that very little pressure from the sword was required to free it.

The massed crowds still waited beyond the palace balcony and the sea of faces looked up at it calling for the young couple. Their patience was rewarded when at 1.30 pm the bride and bridegroom came out to acknowledge their cheers. After a few minutes they were joined by members of their families, including the bridesmaids led by Princess Margaret.

Later that afternoon, Princess Elizabeth and the Duke of Edinburgh left Buckingham Palace in an open landau with escort to drive to a flag bedecked Waterloo Station. From there they journeyed to Broadlands, the Hampshire home of Earl and Countess Mountbatten of Burma, at the start of their honeymoon.

The bride had changed into a love-in-the-mist blue crepe dress worn under a coat in velours cloth to match. Her hat was a bonnet-beret in toning felt, trimmed with an ostrich feather pom-pom with curled quills.

As they drove away they were showered with confetti and rice by the royal guests who followed the carriage out into the forecourt of the palace and watched it turn past the Victoria Memorial between the rows of cheering people.

The vast crowds, who had been so engrossed in the day's events stayed on at the palace until after midnight calling for King George and Queen Elizabeth, who appeared several times on the floodlit balcony.

Whilst on honeymoon, Princess Elizabeth received a letter from her father. With her Majesty's permission, I reproduce an extract.

. . . . I was so proud of you and thrilled at having you so close to me on our long walk in Westminster Abbey, but when I handed your hand to the Archbishop, I felt I had lost something very precious. You were so calm and composed during the Service and said your words with such conviction, that I knew everything was all right. . . .

Right: Engagement day photograph of Princess
Elizabeth and Prince Philip of Greece.
(*Photograph:* Fox Photos)

Inset: The Bride's procession passes down
Whitehall on its way to Westminster Abbey.
(*Photograph:* Radio Times Hulton Picture
Library)

Left: The Archbishop of Canterbury performs the marriage service. (*Photograph:* Fox Photos)

Right: The bridal procession walks down the aisle between the rows of guests. (*Photograph:* Radio Times Hulton Picture Library)

Far Right: The radiant bride and her handsome husband leave the Abbey after their wedding. (*Photograph:* Fox Photos)

Below: The Princess and her husband wave to the cheering crowds as the Glass Coach carries them back to Buckingham Palace for their wedding reception. (*Photograph:* Fox Photos)

ft: At Buckingham Palace after their
dding Princess Elizabeth and Prince Philip
e photographed with the best man, the
desmaids and the two young pages. Also in
e picture are (left to right) Queen Mary,
ncess Andrew of Greece (the groom's
other), the King, the Queen and the
owager Marchioness of Milford Haven.
hotograph: Radio Times Hulton Picture
Library)

ow Left: The royal couple photographed on
e balcony of Buckingham Palace with (left
right) the King, Princess Margaret, Lady
ary Cambridge, the Queen and Queen
ary. (*Photograph:* Keystone Press Agency)

ht: A happy photograph of the newly-weds
Buckingham Palace.
hotograph: Radio Times Hulton Picture
Library)

~MARGARET AND ANTONY~

1936 will be remembered as the year that a royal storm broke over Britain, when it was announced that the King, Edward VIII, intended to abdicate in order to be able to marry the woman with whom he was in love. Parliament and the Church decreed that a marriage between a divorced person and a member of the Royal Family was strictly out of the question. Mrs Wallis Warfield Simpson, an American, was a divorcee. Nonetheless, King Edward was intent on marrying her, despite the fact that Mrs Simpson had made it known publicly that, to save the King from abdicating, she would go away. In December 1936 Edward VIII, King and Emperor, saw no other way of marrying Mrs Simpson, and so signed the Instrument of Abdication. Thus as 'His Royal Highness Prince Edward' he spoke to his former peoples on the evening of 10th December commending to them his brother, the Duke of York, who succeeded him as King George VI. The new King created his elder brother Duke of Windsor, and as such in June 1937, the month after Edward's intended Coronation, he married Mrs Simpson in France.

In London at this time was a six-year-old girl, the youngest daughter of the new king and queen. She was the Princess Margaret Rose. Very rarely does an issue so similar in content arise in royal matters. Yet this was very nearly the case when only eighteen years after the events of 1936, the young Princess Margaret, by now 25 years old, ended the speculation over her romance of some years with a former equerry to her father, Group Captain Peter Townshend. Margaret had fallen in love with the Group Captain when her father was still alive, and Townshend was still in the service of His Majesty. Peter Townshend was the Princess's constant companion. Rumours of a marriage spread like wildfire. However, no matter what one's own opinion on divorce is, the Royal Family are not permitted to marry a divorced person since it is against the Church's teachings. This is what Princess Margaret made reference to in 1955, when in a brief communique she announced that 'being mindful of the Church's teachings . . .' she had decided not to marry the Group Captain. Had she done so, her only option, like that of her uncle, would have been to relinquish her royal style, titles and rights to the Throne, and to live abroad in exile.

For this reason the world was astonished when, five years later, Queen Elizabeth the Queen Mother announced that her younger daughter was to marry. The statement came from Clarence House, home of the Dowager Queen and Princess Margaret, on 26th February 1960.

So closely guarded had been the Princess's romance and courtship with society photographer Mr Antony Armstrong-Jones that few expected it. Who was this man?

He was well known in London's Fleet Street as the photographer who only the year before had taken the 29th birthday studies of his future wife, and who shortly before that had taken official photographs at Buckingham Palace of The Queen, Prince Philip, Prince Charles, Princess Anne and the Duke of Kent.

Antony Charles Robert Armstrong-Jones was born in March 1930, five months before Princess Margaret. He was the son of Ronald Armstrong-Jones, QC, and his wife the former Anne Messell, now Countess of Rosse.

It came as a big enough surprise to learn that Princess Margaret had decided to marry, but it came as an even bigger surprise to learn that her bridegroom was to be a commoner. Her name had been linked with Earls and foreign princes, yet she had found what she was looking for in somebody quite different.

Photographs of Margaret and Antony occupied front and inside pages of national newspapers all over the world. The day after the Queen Mother had made the announcement, the newly betrothed pair posed for photographs at the Royal Lodge, Windsor, the country home of Queen Elizabeth near Windsor Castle. Princess Margaret displayed on her left hand her engagement ring, which was a flower shape of diamonds with a ruby centrepiece.

The engagement caused such a stir that television programmes were interrupted to show the couple arriving at their first engagement together after the announcement. With Queen Elizabeth the Queen Mother, Princess Margaret and her fiancé attended a Gala performance by the Royal Ballet at the Royal Opera House, and upon their arrival they were greeted by a storm of cheering from those who gathered outside as well as the audience inside.

As is usual with Royal weddings, preparations were begun almost immediately, and it was finally announced from the Clarence House press office that the wedding of The Princess Margaret and Mr Antony Armstrong-Jones would take place on the morning of Friday 6th May 1960.

The Queen Mother held a dance at her London home for her

25

daughter and future son-in-law, and included among the guests were the Duke of Kent and Miss Katharine Worsley, who were to marry thirteen months later.

Princess Margaret's wedding would be the first in the Royal Family since that of The Queen thirteen years before.

The Princess chose to be attended by eight small bridesmaids. Taken from her own family and that of Mr Armstrong-Jones, they also came from the families of friends of the Royal Family. They were: The Princess Anne, the bride's niece who would attend her second wedding that year as a bridesmaid; Catherine Vesey, daughter of Armstrong-Jones's sister Susan; Lady Rose Nevill; Miss Sarah Lowther; Miss Annabel Rhodes; Miss Angela Nevill; Lady Virginia Fitzroy, daughter of The Queen's Mistress of the Robes, the Countess of Euston (now the Duchess of Grafton); and Miss Marilyn Wills, the daughter of one of Princess Margaret's Ladies-in-Waiting, the Hon Mrs Wills.

The bridegroom's final choice of best man was Dr Roger Gilliatt. The service would be conducted at Westminster Abbey by the Archbishop of Canterbury, with the assistance of the Dean of Westminster.

As was expected, tens of thousands converged on London for the occasion, and special stands were erected along the processional route to seat those willing to pay astronomical sums for a 'privileged' vantage point. Along the Mall, flying from the triple crowned flag poles, were specially made white silk banners on which, set in a Tudor rose, were the couple's entwined initials in gold, and at the junction of the Mall and the driveway to Clarence House, an immense arch of artificial and real roses was erected. The parks, as if not to be outdone by the Mall decorations, were a blaze of colour with the newly blossoming trees and flower beds.

Taking full advantage of the good weather, the crowds arrived early, as much as two and three days beforehand, to snatch the best possible spots along the processional route. Even more watched the wedding on television: Princess Margaret's was the first to be shown 'live'.

It was arranged that the entire Royal Family would assemble on the morning of 6th May at Buckingham Palace, from where they would drive to the Abbey in carriages. The Queen with Queen Elizabeth the Queen Mother and the Prince of Wales would drive in Queen Alexandra's State Coach (used always at the State Opening of Parliament to convey the Imperial State Crown). Princess Margaret, who would be given away by her brother-in-law, The Duke of Edinburgh, would drive from Clarence House in the Glass Coach, used by all Royal brides in London, and following

the ceremony, she and her husband would drive to Buckingham Palace in the coach for their reception.

The Glass Coach, so called because of its large windows, had been acquired in 1911 for use at the Coronation of King George V. It had originally been built as a Sheriff's Town Coach for the Corporation of London, but when it was discovered that there were not enough coaches for the Coronation processions, the Glass Coach was bought for royal service.

Long before the Royal Family left the palace for the Abbey, the 2000 guests began to arrive. Included in their numbers was Mrs Betty Peabody, a cockney char, who 'did' for Tony Armstrong-Jones at his Pimlico Road home. Her reaction to the invitation – 'Isn't it wonderful?'

At 11.20 am the bridegroom in morning dress arrived with Dr Gilliatt.

As the first of the royal processions formed at the West Door, the chattering of the guests subsided under the strains of a fanfare. The procession, that of the Duchess of Kent (wearing a slim dress of lemon with a matching hat), Princess Alexandra of Kent (wearing acquamarine slipper satin), The Princess Royal (dressed in gold tissue), the Duke of Kent, Prince Michael of Kent and Princess Alice, Countess of Athlone, made its way to the Royal Family's places alongside the High Altar, under the watchful eyes of several television cameras.

Another fanfare shortly afterwards heralded the arrival of Her Majesty The Queen. Her outfit, designed by Norman Hartnell, consisted of a floor length dress made of turquoise blue silk faille with full skirt, over which was worn a short jacket of matching embroidered lace with a hat composed of two large toning roses set on a net base. With The Queen walked Queen Elizabeth the Queen Mother, in a gown of gold with matching gold stole edged with sable and a hat of osprey feathers. With them were the twelve-year-old Prince of Wales, wearing a Royal Stuart Tartan kilt and black velvet jacket, and Queen Ingrid of Denmark, the bride's Godmother, wearing a long dress of ice blue printed silk and a matching feathered hat.

The convoy of cars carrying the eight bridesmaids arrived and they alighted under the awning to await the arrival of Princess Margaret. The youthful group were all wearing replicas of the bride's first ball gown, made of white organza with tiny puffed sleeves and Peter Pan collars and threaded with blue ribbon. On their heads the bridesmaids wore headdresses of white swansdown.

As Princess Margaret arrived, the Kneller Hall Trumpeters broke into another fanfare specially composed by Sir Arthur Bliss and sounded by sixteen trumpets.

Looking nervous and perhaps a little uncertain, the bride smiled briefly at the quips made by the Duke of Edinburgh who was obviously trying very hard to reassure her. At the moment she was to begin her long walk to the altar, the Princess quickly gripped the arm of her brother-in-law, and very slowly the bridal procession moved off.

Princess Margaret, always noted for her love of heavily embroidered outfits, surprised all by her choice of wedding gown which was an essay in complete simplicity. Designed by Hartnell (who took the unusual precaution of taking out a £10,000 Insurance policy to guard against any catastrophe preventing the wedding from taking place), it was made from thirty yards of very fine white silk organza with a 'V' neckline, long tight fitting sleeves caught on the reverse with a row of small buttons, and a very full skirt over several tulle underskirts, almost crinoline in style, made of twelve panels which formed the train. Her hair was another fashion talking point, swept up on either side with a hair piece added to form a coil on top, around which was set an exquisite newly-acquired diamond tiara which secured the full length veil of white silk tulle edged with white organza piping. This fell over the gown in folds forming a train slightly longer than that of the gown. Her Royal Highness had chosen a crescent shaped bouquet made of white orchids and stephanotis.

A ripple of curtseys and bowing heads ran through the congregation as the bride passed along the aisle under the ornate organ screen to the foot of the altar steps where her bridegroom was waiting.

The Dean of Westminster opened the service with those familiar words: 'Dearly beloved we are gathered here in the sight of God. . . .' The vows were taken: 'I, Margaret Rose, take thee, Antony Charles Robert, to my wedded husband. . . .' and the bridegroom placed on the third finger of the bride's left hand a plain wedding ring of Welsh gold. The Archbishop of Canterbury pronounced that they be man and wife together and the Duke of Edinburgh took his seat next to the Queen. Princess Anne, who held the bride's bouquet during the ceremony, stood behind the couple as they moved to the Lord's Table. The remaining bridal attendants sat at the foot of the altar steps.

During the signing of the marriage registers the Choir sang the anthems that the Princess and her fiancé had chosen, and which they had discussed over a glass of sherry with the Dean before the final rehearsal of their wedding on 5th May. The members of the Royal Family, having added their signatures to the Register, returned to their places. Prince Charles turned to the Queen Mother asking if he might keep the programme of his aunt's wedding. His grandmother having reassured him that this was in order, he turned to Queen Ingrid of Denmark to proudly show it off. Another fanfare sounded and the bridegroom led Princess Margaret from the Chapel of St Edward the Confessor, whereupon the usual act of homage to Her Majesty was made. Then, hand in hand, the Princess and Antony Armstrong-Jones made their way back along the central aisle to Purcell's 'Trumpet Tune and Airs' and out into the brilliant daylight.

At Buckingham Palace, Margaret and Antony with their families posed for the official photographs taken by Sir Cecil Beaton in the Throne Room.

While Princess Margaret, her husband and their guests celebrated inside the palace, the immense crowds swarmed towards the building, many breaking through the police cordons to run to the palace railings for the moment the bridal couple would appear on the red and gold draped balcony. When they appeared the crowd roared its approval and Margaret urged Antony to wave. From their vantage point on the balcony the newly married pair saw nothing but a vast sea of people as far as the bottom of the Mall. Shortly afterwards the entire Royal Family, together with Armstrong-Jones's parents, Ronald Armstrong-Jones and the Countess of Rosse, joined them to the acclaim of the crowds.

Although The Queen had declared 6th May a holiday for schoolchildren, there were far more adults than children in evidence along the routes taken by the Princess and her husband on their wedding day. Those who did work on that day flooded into the streets of the City as the couple, in an open topped Rolls-Royce, drove from Buckingham Palace to the Pool of London, from where they sailed in the Royal Yacht *Britannia* to the Caribbean for their honeymoon.

The Queen and members of the Royal Family had followed the car out into the forecourt of the Palace, throwing confetti and rice and waving farewell. Slowly the car made its way through the cheering throngs of people up past the Tower of London to where the Royal Yacht, put at their disposal by Her Majesty, was berthed. The crowds, anxious to catch a glimpse of the Princess and her husband, pushed towards the car and halted it several times. On its return to the Palace, a sum of two hundred pounds was spent on re-spraying the vehicle. It had become badly scratched due to the crowds pressing forward, and one enterprising onlooker settled for nothing less than taking a knife to the maroon bodywork to carve the couple's initials, framed by a heart and completed with an arrow.

Arriving sometime after schedule, Princess Margaret, now wearing a coat of sunshine yellow silk over a sheath dress to match of yellow organdie and wearing a hat of stiffened tulle dotted with tiny string like bows, boarded the royal barge with her husband. The barge took them out to the Royal Yacht, which was brilliant with flags; from the main mast was flying the Princess's personal standard.

Small craft and barges hooted a welcome as the Yacht slipped anchor and the vast blue and white royal vessel glided down the Thames, the arms of Tower Bridge opening to allow the yacht through. Her Royal Highness and Mr Armstrong-Jones stood on the bridge waving to the crowds clustered along the river bank and at garden fences at the edge of the Thames. All was set for their six week honeymoon, which the press termed a 'calypso honeymoon'.

ove: Princess Alexandra arrives for her cousin's wedding. Behind Prince Richard of Gloucester and Prince Michael of Kent. *otograph:* Fox Photos)

Above: Her Majesty the Queen arrives at the Abbey with Queen Elizabeth the Queen Mother, and Prince Charles. (*Photograph:* Fox Photos)

Left: Queen Ingrid of Denmark whispers * Prince Charles. Behind is the Duchess of ?oucester. (*Photograph:* Fox Photos)

?t: Princess Margaret steps down from the ?ass Coach at the West Door of the Abbey. (*Photograph:* Fox Photos)

?ht: Princess Anne, one of the eight ?desmaids, arrives at Westminster Abbey. (*Photograph:* Fox Photos)

Right: A radiant Princess Margaret with * brother-in-law, Prince Philip, drives to * Abbey. (*Photograph:* Fox Photos)

?ow: The Princess in her exquisite wedding ?wn is escorted by Prince Philip into the ?bey. (*Photograph:* Fox Photos)

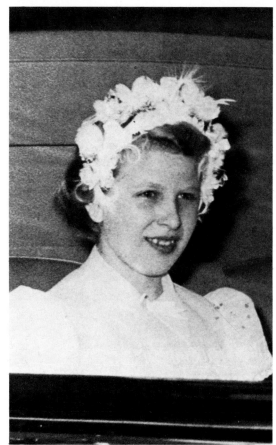

ft: The bridal pair walk down the aisle
tween the rows of guests.

(*Photograph:* Fox Photos)

Opposite below left and right: Antony
Armstrong-Jones helps his wife with the
complicated task of getting her voluminous
dress into the confined space of their carriage.

(*Photographs:* Fox Photos)

Below: The coach returns to Buckingham
Palace for the reception.

(*Photograph:* Fox Photos)

Above Left: The happy bridal couple wave t the crowds from the balcony of Buckinghar Palace. (*Photograph:* Fox Photos)

Left: A beautiful study by Cecil Beaton of Princess Margaret in her wedding gown in Throne Room at Buckingham Palace.
(*Photograph:* Cecil Beaton, Camera Pr

Above: The bride's mother and sister wave farewell as the couple leave for their honeymoon. (*Photograph:* Fox Photos)

Above Right: Their car speeds through the patient throngs of well-wishers.
(*Photograph:* Fox Phot

Right: Princess Margaret and Mr Armstrong-Jones with the best man, Roger Gilliatt, and the bridesmaids.
(*Photograph:* Keystone Press Ager

~KATHARINE AND EDWARD~

'I, Katharine Lucy Mary, take thee, Edward George Nicholas Paul Patrick, to my wedded husband, to have and to hold from this day forward....'

From Squire's daughter, kindergarten teacher and assistant in a Canadian jewellery store, to Her Royal Highness The Duchess of Kent. This was the destiny of Miss Katharine Worsley, only daughter of the late Sir William Worsley of Hovingham Hall, Yorkshire, former Lord Lieutenant of the North Riding, and his wife Joyce Morgan Brunner, daughter of Sir John Fowler Brunner, Baronet.

Katharine Worsley, third Royal Duchess of Kent, is a descendant of an ancient family who have been land owners in the North Riding of Yorkshire since the reign of Elizabeth I. The family's roots were then in Lancashire, their name coming from Worsley in that county. The family had been lords there since the time of the Normans. Worsley subsequently became a suburb of Manchester. The two most important branches of the Worsley family left Lancashire in Tudor times, establishing their respective branches in the Isle of Wight and at Hovingham in Yorkshire. Both received baronetcies. One branch of the family was founded by James Worsley, who was Keeper of the Wardrobe to King Henry VIII. He appointed Worsley to the post of Governor of the Isle of Wight. Though this family is now extinct in the male line it is represented in present times by the family of the Earl of Yarborough, whose son bears the courtesy title of Lord Worsley.

One of Katharine's ancestors was Sir Robert Worsley, who acquired the manor of Hovingham in the year 1563. The house was rebuilt during the reign of King George III by the Member of Parliament for Calne, Wiltshire, Thomas Worsley, who was also Riding Master to George III. Thomas Worsley's grandson was Sir William Worsley who received the baronetcy from Queen Victoria in 1838. Miss Worsley is also able to boast descent from Oliver Cromwell, the Lord Protector, through another distant ancestor, Elizabeth, Lady Frankland, a granddaughter of Cromwell.

Katharine Worsley's father, Sir William, who died in the early part of 1974, was the 4th baronet. Katharine was the couple's fifth child and only daughter and was born in Yorkshire on 22nd February 1933.

His Royal Highness Prince Edward, Duke of Kent, elder son of the late George, Duke of Kent and Marina, Princess of Greece and Denmark, grandson of King George V and Queen Mary and first cousin of the present Queen was born on 9th October 1935. He succeeded to the dukedom of Kent at the early age of eight years, on the tragic and untimely death of his father in a flying accident while on active service in 1942.

A soldier in the Royal Scots Greys, he was to meet his future wife, who is two years his senior, at her home during a dance given by Sir William and Lady Worsley.

The romance of the Duke of Kent and Katharine Worsley was a closely guarded secret and it was said that whenever they were to meet, the Duke would always arrive with a chosen friend of Miss Worsley's and she would arrive alone by taxi. Princess Marina, the Duke's mother, and the Royal Family had met and approved of his attractive girl friend and on 8th March 1961, Princess Marina, via the Court Circular, announced the betrothal of her son to Miss Worsley, to which union The Queen had gladly given her consent.

The setting for the wedding was finally decided upon—York Minster, which is some twenty miles from the bride's home at Hovingham Hall. The date was set for Thursday 8th June 1961. All would have to be arranged in exactly three months from the announcement of the couple's engagement. The Queen had signified that she would not object to travelling to York for the wedding, and indeed she and other members of the Royal Family would travel from London aboard the Royal train, and most of the processions to the Minster on the afternoon of the wedding would start from the railway station.

For Yorkshire and the Minster itself it was an unforgettable occasion. Only once before in the Minster's entire history had a Royal Wedding taken place there. That had occurred in 1328, some 633 years previously, when King Edward III had married Phillipa of Hainault. As with the marriage of Princess Margaret and Antony Armstrong-Jones the previous year, the ceremony was to be broadcast and televised live.

Princess Marina, always noted for her elegance, recommended that her future daughter in law should commission John Cavanagh to design and make the bridal gown. He had for some time been making exclusive outfits for the Princess and had in fact started in the couture business at the age of 17 picking up pins in the employment of Captain Edward Molyneux, who had made Marina's bridal outfit in 1934. Cavanagh eventually became

Molyneux's principal assistant. As his own business developed, Cavanagh had major successes with his fashion shows in the USA and Canada. His first ambition of establishing his own *salon* realised, in 1966 he opened a ready-to-wear shop next door to his *salon* at 26 Curzon Street, and later still created complete wardrobes for such people as Lady Soames (the former Mary Churchill, daughter of Sir Winston). In 1970 Princess Anne took a selection of Cavanagh outfits with her when she visited Australia and New Zealand.

Cavanagh made five sketches of wedding gowns for the future Duchess of Kent and discussed each of them with her and Princess Marina.

The design chosen, it was now up to him to find the ideal fabric, which he in fact found in France. When he brought a sample of the material back to London, both Katharine and Marina agreed that it was exactly what was needed.

Mr Cavanagh described the chosen fabric as 'white silk gauze with a pearlised motif'. The design was basically a simple one – roll neckline, long fitted sleeves caught at the wrist with a row of tiny buttons, a full skirt over several similarly full underskirts, forming a long train edged with white satin ribbon. There was a longer over-train from the waist. During one fitting of the wedding dress, the bride and Princess Marina expressed some concern at the length and volume of the train which was in fact some fifteen feet in length. The designer was quick to explain that not unnaturally in the limited space of a work room the train would indeed appear immense, but once inside York Minster with its vast interior, the train would scale down perfectly. Both Katharine and the Princess were thus persuaded not to alter the train at all.

Movement was found to be restricted because the train, although of a light fabric, would pull her back particularly when the time came at the conclusion of the ceremony for the bride to make the customary curtsey to the Queen. Katharine tried this movement during a fitting and it was found that she would be unable to turn to face the Queen as the pull on her train restricted the necessary movement. It was finally resolved that the bride would half turn towards Her Majesty and then step back into the folds of the gown, thus loosening the strain behind and giving her the freedom she required to perfect her act of homage. During fittings of the gown, Miss Worsley not only practiced her curtsey, using the arm of Mr Cavanagh for support, but also knelt on stacks of telephone directories, so that any minor alterations could be made, again to give the bride maximum freedom when she had to kneel and stand unaided.

The gown was made in a room set aside in Cavanagh's Mayfair salon. To ensure security a steel plated door was installed and kept locked at all times. The three seamstresses working exclusively on the gown burned all snippets of the material not being used. In all, only eight people worked on the creation: the head saleswoman, the fitter, the stockkeeper, the three seamstresses, the designer and his assistant. Eventually, a ninth person was let in on the secret, the future Duchess's milliner, since he would have the job of arranging the bridal veil.

There were to be eight bridesmaids: The Princess Anne, Diana Worsley, Emily Briggs, Sandra Butter, Joanna Fitzroy, Katharine Ashley Cooper and Willa Worsley. The three young page boys were Simon Hay, Edward Beckett and William Worsley.

On the morning of 8th June the guests began to take their places within the Minster. One of the guests that day was Mrs Elsie Cobb, who for twenty five years had been the Matron of a York children's home where the bride had worked at the age of 19. 'It was a wonderful surprise to be invited,' she told reporters. 'I am very thrilled. Katharine was a great help to us when she was here. The children idolised her and she was kindness itself to them.'

As protocol demands, the less important members of the Royal Family arrived first, including Earl Mountbatten of Burma with his two daughters Patricia, Baroness Brabourne and the Lady Pamela Hicks, and the Earl of Harewood with his former wife Marion (now Mrs Jeremy Thorpe). Foreign Royal guests followed: The Crown Prince Harald of Norway, the Crown Prince Constantine of Greece, Princess Irene of the Netherlands, Prince Tomislav of Yugoslavia, Prince and Princess Frederick of Prussia, Prince and Princess Georg of Denmark and Prince and Princess Alexander of Yugoslavia.

The senior members of the Royal Family then arrived: H M Queen Elizabeth the Queen Mother, wearing pale blue, with Queen Victoria Eugenie of Spain (a daughter of Queen Victoria's daughter Vicky); Princess Margaret, in an ice blue silk duster coat and matching halo hat, and Antony Armstrong-Jones; the Princess Royal; the Duke and Duchess of Gloucester with their elder son Prince William; Princess Alice, Countess of Athlone; the bridegroom's mother in champagne coloured organza embroidered with gold, and the bridegroom's sister, Princess Alexandra, wearing an outfit of azalea pink; and then The Queen arrived in a lilac silk outfit with The Duke of Edinburgh and The Prince of Wales.

The bridegroom, who had been given special permission by the War Office to wear the famous old scarlet and blue ceremonial uniform of the Royal Scots Greys (his own regiment), had already arrived with his Best Man, Prince Michael. The Duke's uniform was last worn ceremonially after the First World War.

Finally the trumpet fanfares sounded the bride's arrival; the sharp notes echoed through the ancient building, and Katharine, looking a little nervous, began her long stately walk down the aisle on the arm of her father. The wedding dress shimmered as she walked, the long train flowing out behind her in sculptured folds. On her head she wore a diamond bandeaux, securing her long crisp white silk net veil. Over her face, two sections of veiling were caught with pins; these were to be removed during the signing of the Register. Her bouquet was composed of yellow roses and heather.

The bridesmaids followed, wearing long white dresses decorated with tiny yellow rosebuds and their youthful hairstyles enhanced by yellow rosebuds dotted all over.

As the bridal procession made its way slowly along the Nave towards the Altar, Sir Hubert Parry's hymn 'Laudare Dominum' was sung by the choir.

With the bride and bridegroom in position before the altar, the service commenced. The form was taken from the 1928 Prayer book which omits the word 'obey', but at the request of the bride, who wanted to promise to obey her husband, the word was included.

At 2.50 pm the Archbishop of York pronounced Katharine and Edward man and wife and they knelt in prayer.

While the registers were being signed, the anthem 'Lord who has made us for thine own' was sung. Also included in the service was one of the bride's favourite prayers, attributed to St Francis of Assisi. The words are as follows:

'Lord, make us instruments of thy Will:
Where there is hate, may we bring love;
Where there is offence, may we bring pardon;
Where there is discord, may we bring peace;
Where there is error, may we bring truth;
Where there is doubt, may we bring faith;
Where there is despair, may we bring hope;
Where there is darkness, may we bring light;
Where there is sadness, may we bring joy;

O Master, make us seek not so much to be
consoled as to console; to be understood as
to understand; to be loved as to love. For
it is in giving that we receive; in self-
forgetfulness that we find; in pardoning
that we are pardoned, in dying that
we shall wake to life Eternal;
where thou livest and reignest in the
glory of the blessed Trinity one God
World without end.'

The hymn 'O Perfect Love' then followed, and the bride and bridegroom began to make their way from the Minster while the organ played the delightfully bright 'Toccata in F' by Widor. The girl who had arrived a commoner was now a Royal Duchess.

All had gone without a hitch, including the new Duchess's deep and graceful curtsey to The Queen.

The Duke and his bride moved slowly down the aisle, out under the specially erected awning and under an arch of swords furnished by the Duke's fellow officers.

After the long drive back to Hovingham Hall, the reception for the two thousand guests was held on the lawns of the house where multi-coloured marquees had been erected. The wedding cake was cut by the newly married pair using the Duke's sword. Then it was time to change, the new Duchess of Kent into a sapphire blue silk coat over a printed silk dress with a green petal hat to match, and the Duke into a grey lounge suit. Following farewells from the Queen and the members of their families, the bridal pair drove to RAF Linton where a Heron of The Queen's Flight was waiting to fly them to Scotland and The Queen Mother's house on the Balmoral estate, Birkhall, at the start of a honeymoon that was concluded in Spain.

Those who were gathered at the airfield watched as the bright pink aircraft soared 8000 feet up into the sky, and, upon the couple's arrival in Aberdeen, it seemed as though nearly all the inhabitants had come out into the streets to cheer them on their way and to throw handfuls of confetti.

Right: The marriage service is performed in the august surroundings of York Minster.
(Photograph: Fox Photo

Below: The bride arrives at the Minster on t
arm of her father, Sir William Worsley.
(Photograph: Fox Photo

Above: The Duke bows and Katharine make a graceful obeisance to Her Majesty the Que while other members of the Royal Family look on. (*Photograph:* Keystone Press Agency

Left: The newly-weds pass the Royal Family on their way down the aisle.
(*Photograph:* Fox Photo

Right: The Duke and his new Duchess are followed in procession by the pages and bridesmaids. (*Photograph:* Fox Pho

Left: The newly-weds walk beneath the crossed swords of the Duke's Regiment, the Royal Scots Greys.
(*Photograph:* Keystone Press Agency)

Right: A charming close-up of the happy couple. (*Photograph:* Fox Photos)

~ALEXANDRA AND ANGUS~

The announcement that Princess Alexandra of Kent was to marry was greeted with a great deal of excitement and enthusiasm by the British people.

The release of the formal statement by Princess Marina, Duchess of Kent, came on 29th November 1962. Twenty-eight years before, on that date, the former Princess Marina of Greece and Denmark, daughter of Prince and Princess Nicholas of Greece, had been married at Westminster Abbey to HRH Prince George, Duke of Kent, fourth son of King George V and Queen Mary.

From her mother, Princess Alexandra inherited an enormous amount of Imperial history. Princess Marina's father was the third son of King George I and Queen Olga of Greece, and her mother was the former Grand Duchess Helen of Russia, daughter of the Grand Duke Vladimir, a younger brother of Tsar Alexander III of All the Russias.

The future husband of Princess Marina's only daughter was the Honourable Angus Ogilvy, a successful company director, born the second son of the Earl and Countess of Airlie. Princess Marina had said she was delighted. She had known the Airlie family for many years.

The Airlie family had been friends of the British Royal Family for a considerable time, and indeed Angus's grandmother, Mabell, Countess of Airlie had been a close friend and Lady in Waiting to Queen Mary for over fifty years. His father had been Lord Chamberlain to Queen Elizabeth the Queen Mother, an appointment he assumed in 1937, the year of her Coronation. Angus Ogilvy's sister in law, the present Countess of Airlie, is now an extra Lady in Waiting to Queen Elizabeth II.

Alexandra Helen Elizabeth Olga Christabel, the couple's second child, had been born to the Duke and Duchess of Kent on Christmas Day 1936. Their first, Prince Edward, the present Duke of Kent, had been born in 1935 the year before and Prince Michael was born in 1942, shortly before his father's tragic death in a flying accident.

The children of the Duke and Duchess of Kent were the first members of the Royal Family to be educated at public schools—the Princess attended Heathfield—and this may well be one of the causes of the Princess's popularity.

It would seem that every so often, particularly if a 'royal' issue comes to the fore, a popularity poll is taken and invariably Alexandra's name comes out very near the top. It would not be mere flattery to say that her popularity is because she is a very modest woman. A lady linked with the Princess has said that it is probably her sincere interest in people from every walk of life that makes her one of the most popular Royal figures today. Alexandra dislikes red tape and has always opted for simplicity, an admirable quality in a person holding the position of a royal princess.

The Honourable Angus James Bruce Ogilvy, the man Princess Alexandra was to marry, was born on 14th September 1928, eight years before the Princess. He was educated at Heatherdown, near Ascot, and at Eton. He was commissioned in the Scots Guards, and is in fact now on the Reserve of Officers. In 1948 Angus went to Trinity College, Oxford where he read modern Greats, philosophy, politics and economics.

In 1950, Mr Ogilvy joined the large Drayton organisation, which is one of the largest investment trusts in the City of London. Like Princess Alexandra, he is connected with several charitable organisations and he is a member of the Royal Company of Archers, which is The Queen's Bodyguard for Scotland.

The history of the Ogilvy family is full of the bloody battles and feuds which are an inescapable part of the history of the Scottish clans.

Born the son of the 12th Earl of Airlie, Angus Ogilvy is descended directly in the male line from Gillebride, the earliest known Earl of Angus, who was one of the leaders in the wars of King William the Lion of Scotland against England. The kingdom of Angus lay between the North Esk and the Tay on the Eastern seaboard. When Angus became a province of Scotland, after the country had been united into one kingdom, it came under a powerful family, the Mormaers, who became Earls of Angus.

In about 1176, King William the Lion gave the lands of Ogilvy to Gilbert, a younger son of Earl Gillebride, and thus originated the surname of the Ogilvy family, once spelt Ogguluin.

In 1432, King James I granted a Licence to Sir Walter Ogilvy, High Treasurer of Scotland, to convert his Tower of Airlie into a castle. In 1491 James IV created Sir James Ogilvy Lord of Airlie and, as such, the King made him Ambassador to the Danish Royal Court.

The legend of the Airlie drummer, who is said to be heard beating his drums as a warning of impending death in the Ogilvy

55

family, is attributed to the following facts. In 1639, King Charles I created James, 7th Lord Ogilvy, Earl of Airlie, and not a year after the accolade had been bestowed upon him, the Earl's family seat, Airlie Castle, was razed to the ground by the Marquess of Argyll and his associates, leaving the Earl with 'not in all his lands a cock to crow day'.

The drummer, a member of the Cameron clan, was said to have been posted on a look out tower, and to have been left to burn to death in the belief that he had betrayed the castle. Hence, one would assume as a token to re-affirm his loyalty, his ghost remains to beat the drums as a warning of a death within the Ogilvy family.

Airlie Castle was subsequently rebuilt on a smaller scale and the Airlie family seat is now Cortachy Castle, with Airlie Castle as the Dower House.

Angus Ogilvy is also a distant kinsman of the present Queen, via her mother, Elizabeth, since in 1696 David, 3rd Earl of Airlie, was married to the Lady Grizel Lyons, daughter of Patrick, 3rd Earl of Strathmore.

The Queen was duly informed of her cousin's intention to marry, and the formal wording of the betrothal announcement in the Court Circular was concluded with the words: '. . . to which union the Queen has gladly given her consent.'

Princess Alexandra and Angus Ogilvy had been friends for some years, and in fact had met over eight years before their engagement was announced. Three months after they had become officially engaged, it was disclosed from Princess Marina's office that the marriage of Her Royal Highness Princess Alexandra of Kent and the Honourable Angus Ogilvy would take place on the morning of Wednesday 24th April 1963 at 12 noon at Westminster Abbey.

The mammoth task of arranging the wedding was undertaken by the Lord Chamberlain's Department at St James's Palace and the Private Secretary's office at Kensington Palace in conjunction with Princess Marina's Press department.

Among those who received the official invitations were British and Foreign persons, High Commissioners and Ambassadors, and representatives of the organisations under the patronage and presidency of Her Royal Highness the Bride.

Like her sister in law, the present Duchess of Kent, Princess Alexandra asked Mayfair *couturière* John Cavanagh to design and make her wedding gown. Both Alexandra and her mother saw Mr Cavanagh at their apartments at Kensington Palace to discuss the type of bridal gown that was desired. It was established from the start that Alexandra wanted lace, in a simple, uncluttered style. It was once written that the Princess had always favoured simple well cut outfits because she disliked the fuss of bows and buttons and unnecessary decoration.

The late Lady Patricia Ramsay, the former Princess Patricia of Connaught, had given her bridal veil of lace to Princess Alexandra, and the Princess liked the design of oak leaves and acorns and wanted to know if it would be possible to reproduce the motif on the lace for her own wedding attire.

Taking the old rectangular bridal veil with him, Mr Cavanagh left for France to see if it would be possible to reproduce the design for the Princess. There he found a small company in the north able to complete the task, and it was finally reproduced in no less than eighty yards of the finest magnolia tinted lace.

Special arrangements were made with the British Customs and Excise Department to clear the parcel when it arrived in England. Despite the cooperation of the department, the designer was not particularly happy that it would have to be declared as lace for the royal wedding dress. The Press seem to develop a sixth sense when it comes to events such as royal weddings and will not unnaturally pull out all the stops for a royal scoop. The merest hint that Princess Alexandra was to wear lace would have spoiled the surprise because, as with all royal weddings dresses, details are kept secret until an appointed time on the day of the wedding.

Princess Alexandra was a regular visitor to Mr Cavanagh's salon in Curzon Street, very often dashing in for fittings just after the offices had been closed for the day.

To add the merest shimmer as the bride walked in the Abbey under the glare of television lights, an underdress sewn with thousands of gold sequins was to be worn under the wedding gown itself.

The original idea was for the dress to be completed by a full court train falling from the shoulders, with a veil of tulle over that. However, one evening during a visit to the salon with her mother, Princess Alexandra was standing before a full length mirror wearing the creation, with the designer standing behind her holding the proposed train, when he suggested that the train could easily be worn as the bridal veil. Both the bride and Princess Marina thought this a splendid idea; it would be the first time that a Royal bride had worn a perfectly matching wedding gown and veil.

To add the finishing touch to the outfit, Princess Alexandra gave to her dressmaker a length of old Valenciennes lace which had belonged to her grandmother, Princess Nicholas of Greece. Mr Cavanagh decided against having the fabric dry cleaned, and, following a thorough hand wash, it became the shade of the remainder of the bridal material. The Valenciennes lace thus formed the edging of the Princess's veil.

On the morning of the wedding the Royal Family made their way in order of importance to Westminster Abbey, and The Queen's Rolls-Royce arrived at the white pillared entrance to Kensington Palace to collect the Bride. The maroon body-work of the Queen's State car gleamed in the weak sunlight, and the hood was removed, as on all similar occasions, to afford a perfect view of the Princess as she drove to her wedding.

The television cameras were at the door to record the moment Princess Alexandra stepped out. As she did so, the door of the limousine was opened and she was assisted into it and her voluminous train, some twenty one feet in length, arranged about her. On her head, securing the veil, the bride wore a diamond tiara loaned by Princes Marina, who had worn it at her wedding in 1934, and which had been then a gift of the City of London. The bridal bouquet, made by the firm of Longmans, was in the shape of a victorian posy composed of white freesias, white narcissi and small stephanotis blooms.

Seated beside his sister was the Duke of Kent. He and the Duchess had flown to England from Hong Kong, where he was stationed with his regiment, to give his only sister away. As the Rolls-Royce drove slowly down the palace driveway into Kensington High Street, the traffic was halted for a short time to allow the small bridal procession to pass unhindered.

The car, displaying the royal crown above the windscreen, drove along to the Alexandra Gate of Hyde Park, along the carriageway to Hyde Park Corner, through the centre of the Wellington Arch, down Constitution Hill and the Mall and then along the remainder of the royal processional route to the West Door of Westminster Abbey. There the group of bridal attendants awaited the bride's arrival. The attendants numbered seven – five bridesmaids and two page-boys. They were: The Princess Anne (looking very sophisticated for her twelve years, with her hair swept-up for the first time); The Archduchess Elisabeth of Austria, daughter of Archduke and Archduchess Ferdinand of Austria; Doune Ogilvy; Georgina Butter; Emma Tennant; The Master of Ogilvy; and Simon Hay.

The Bridegroom who had arrived with his best-man, the Hon Peregrine Fairfax, sat in their appointed seats in front of those of the Royal Family. The guests came from all over Europe, and among them were: Queen Ingrid of Denmark with her younger daughter the Princess Anne-Marie, who was to marry King Constantine of the Hellenes little more than a year later; Queen Louise of Sweden; the former Queen Helen of Rumania; Queen Frederika of the Hellenes with her two daughters, Princess Sophia, who in the previous May had married Don Juan Carlos of Spain in Athens, and

who is now The Princess of Spain, and Princess Irene (now an accomplished concert pianist); Prince Paul of Yugoslavia with his wife Princess Olga, sister of Princess Marina; King Olav of Norway with his son, the Crown Prince Harald; Queen Victoria-Eugenie (Queen Ena) of Spain, a granddaughter of Queen Victoria and the Prince Consort; and Princess Desiree of Sweden.

All was now ready within the Abbey for the arrival of the Bride. As she stepped out of her car, the immense train was set straight; the bride took the arm of her brother and smiling broadly, yet looking a little nervous, prepared for the long slow walk towards the High Altar. The Princess and her fiancé together had chosen most of the music for the wedding, and a welcoming fanfare was followed by the first of the processional music, the hymn 'Glory, glory, glory, Lord God Almighty'. The procession, headed by the Cross of Westminster and the Clergy, moved on its way down the length of the blue carpeted aisle.

The Queen, wearing a Hartnell ensemble of palest green organza, her dress embroidered with a large lily-of-the-valley motif to match her close fitting hat of the same flowers, stood beside the Duke of Edinbugh. The Prince of Wales, attending his third Royal Wedding, stood beside his father and grandmother, Queen Elizabeth the Queen Mother, the latter wearing an outfit of silver lace over bluebell tulle, with a striking hat of osprey feathers. Then came the bride's mother, Princess Marina, Duchess of Kent, wearing a shimmering tunic dress of gold tissue over an underskirt embroidered in topaz and gold and, to match, a wide brimmed Cavalier style hat, covered with gold sequins and adorned with a large diamond and pearl drop brooch. This contrasted sharply with the outfit worn by the latest of the royal brides, her daughter in law, The Duchess of Kent, who favoured a coral pink dress and coat, worn with a coolie style hat, again in coral pink. Another eye catching outfit was worn by Princess Margaret, who sat with Lord Snowdon. Margaret's outfit consisted of a pale lemon sheath dress worn under an organdie coat covered with silk primroses, and a yellow toque hat, tilted slightly forward with her dark hair brushed over the brim at the back.

As the bride approached, Angus Ogilvy and his best man stepped forward. The bridal procession made a dramatic picture, with the bride's train cascading in sculptured folds and followed by the bridesmaids and pages. The two page-boys held hands with the small bridesmaids, one trio behind the other, under the watchful eye of Princess Anne who, as chief bridesmaid, was to receive the bride's bouquet.

John Cavanagh had also been responsible for the making of the attendants' outfits. There were the pages in kilts, white silk shirts and lace jabots, and the bridesmaids in long dresses of creamy-white Ziberline (a fabric slightly heavier than silk) with rounded necklines, trumpet sleeves, and matching bandeaux headdresses also made of Ziberline. All the girls carried miniature replicas of the bride's bouquet.

The Dean of Westminster, Dr Eric S Abbott, stepped forward to open the service, which was exactly the same as the bride's mother's; the Introduction and the final prayers being said from the 1928 Prayer Book, the central section and the marriage vows being taken from the 1662 Prayer book, which includes the promise to 'obey'. Then the Archbishop of Canterbury, Dr Michael Ramsay, addressed the couple. Princess Alexandra's was his first Royal wedding since he became Primate of All England.

The responses of Princess Alexandra and her bridegroom were heard very clearly; the Archbishop then pronounced that they be man and wife together and, after the Blessing, the bride and bridegroom approached the High Altar and the 37th Psalm was sung by the choir. Prayers were said by the Precentor and a blessing followed by the Dean of Westminster.

The Abbey choristers sang the anthem 'God be in my Head'. In the absence of a sermon or address, the 13th Chapter of the 1st Epistle of St Paul to the Corinthians was read by the Vicar of Kensington, followed by the wedding hymn 'Love divine all loves excelling'.

As with all weddings, religious and civil, there then followed the signing of the marriage Registers in the Chapel of St Edward the Confessor by the Princess and her husband and members of their immediate families. The final touch of formality dispensed with, Princess Alexandra, now known as Her Royal Highness Princess Alexandra, the Hon Mrs Angus Ogilvy, left the chapel on the arm of her husband to Widor's 'Toccata in F' and both paid homage to The Queen – the Princess making a deep curtsey to Her Majesty and Mr Ogilvy bowing his head.

From the Abbey, the bride and bridegroom travelled in the Glass Coach along the processional route to their wedding breakfast at St James's Palace in the Mall. The Glass Coach was escorted by a travelling party of the Household Cavalry.

At St James's Palace, the official wedding photographs were posed for in the crimson, gold and white Throne Room, and during the arrangements for the group photographs, Princess Anne proudly displayed the inscribed gold bracelet which the bridegroom had given to her, and Princess Margaret helped to arrange her cousin's immense train.

The wedding cake, standing five feet high and weighing 130 pounds, bore the arms of the Princess and her husband, and replicas of bagpipes were also added at the request of Princess Alexandra.

Following the reception, the bride and 'groom left for Scotland on the first part of their honeymoon. Like Princess Alexandra's brother and sister in law, the Ogilvys were to fly first to Scotland to stay at the Queen Mother's Highland home, Birkhall, and then they were to fly on to Spain to conclude their honeymoon in Marbella. They left St James's to a barrage of cheers, rice and confetti. The bride wore a skirt and jacket of bright flamingo pink jersey wool with a cream silk blouse, and a hat of pink shantung silk in turban style, with beige crocodile skin accessories.

Tied to the back of the dark blue Rolls-Royce belonging to Princes Marina, in which the newly married pair travelled with police escort to Heathrow Airport, was a good luck token of a small bootee fixed to a tartan ribbon.

Thanked for their courtesy to the press, Princess Alexandra replied: '. . . the ordeal for us is now over. . . but we do want to thank everyone for being so kind'.

ve: Princess Alexandra with her husband, Angus Ogilvy, walk
n the aisle of Westminster Abbey after their marriage.

(*Photograph:* Fox Photos)

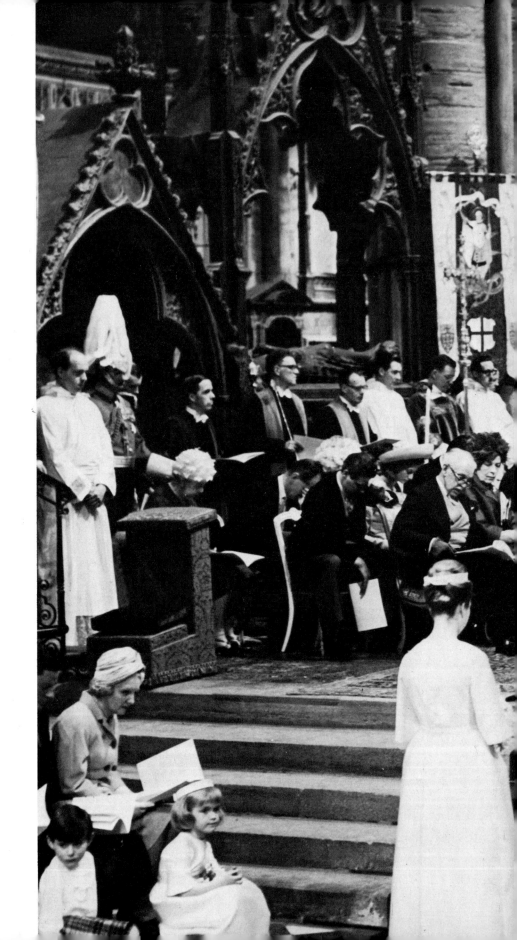

Right: The Dean of Westminster, who assisted the Archbishop of Canterbury, performs part of the marriage service while the couple kneel at the altar. Princess Anne, the chief bridesmaid, stands at the foot of the steps.

(*Photograph:* Fox Photos)

*: The newly-weds, looking happy and
xed, smile at their guests as they leave the
ey. (*Photograph:* Keystone Press Agency)

t: A beautiful study of the radiant bride
her new husband.
     (*Photograph:* Keystone Press Agency)

w: The Glass Coach carries the Princess
Mr Ogilvy from the Abbey to St James's
ce for their wedding reception.
           (*Photograph:* Fox Photos)

Below: With the bride and groom and their attendants are (left to right) the Countess of Airlie, Princess Marina, the Earl of Airlie and the Hon Peregrine Fairfax, the best man. Princess Anne, standing at the bride's left hand, looks elegant as the chief bridesmaid.

(*Photograph:* Keystone Press Agency)

ght: Princess Anne follows the couple as
y leave the Abbey.

(*Photograph:* Fox Photos)

ow: A smiling Princess Alexandra is driven
th her husband from St James's Palace at
* start of their honeymoon.

(*Photograph:* Fox Photos)

~RICHARD AND BIRGITTE~

The Duke and Duchess of Gloucester had been in the public eye for several decades since their Buckingham Palace wedding in November 1935. Their sons, however, have been relatively unknown to the public, since both chose to follow their own careers and neither participated frequently in the royal round.

Consequently, Prince Richard came into the news when in February 1972 his engagement to Miss Birgitte Van Deurs was formally announced by the Duke and Duchess of Gloucester.

As a partner in a City based firm of Architects, it seemed that Richard would be able to continue in what could be termed a 'private existence', assisting in royal engagements when the occasion demanded.

The Prince's elder brother, William, himself never one for publicity, featured briefly in the press during the early part of the summer of 1972 when a romance between himself and Mrs Nicole Sieff, former wife of a wealthy businessman, became news. All came suddenly to an end when, one month after the marriage of Prince Richard, William was tragically killed while piloting his own light aircraft. The Prince was 30.

With the death of his brother, Prince Richard took one step further up the ladder of succession, automatically becoming heir to his father. He succeeded to the Dukedom in June 1974.

Richard Alexander Walter George of Gloucester was born on 26th August 1944, nine years after his parents' marriage. His education began at Eton and was later completed at Magdalene College, Cambridge, where he gained his BA. Unlike some titles now adopted by the Royal House, the Dukedom of Gloucester (like that of York) has always been a Royal title.

King Richard II created his uncle Thomas Plantaganet (known as Thomas of Woodstock and sixth son of King Edward III) Duke of Gloucester in 1385. On the Duke's death in 1387, Gloucester was granted as an earldom to Humphrey Plantaganet, fourth son of King Henry IV, who died in 1447.

The third Duke of Gloucester, who was given the title in 1461, was Richard Crookback, afterwards King Richard III. Thus the title merged with the Crown.

In 1659 King Charles II, while in exile, made his brother Henry Duke of Gloucester but, as he died a bachelor in 1660, his honours became extinct. The title did not appear again until 1764, and then as a Peerage dignity when King George III created his brother

William Henry Duke of Gloucester and Edinburgh. He was succeeded by his son, William Frederick, who died in 1834, when the dukedom again became extinct. It remained thus until the late Duke, Prince Henry, became the title holder.

If little was known of Prince Richard, even less information was to hand about Britain's newest princess. In August 1973, the Central Office of Information compiled and released a brief biography of the wife of Prince Richard, headed simply HRH PRINCESS RICHARD OF GLOUCESTER. Born in Odense, Denmark on 20th June 1946, the Princess was educated at Odense, at Brillantmont, Lausanne in Switzerland and at the Niels Brock Commercial College in Copenhagen. She attended a language school in Cambridge, England, and this is in fact when she first met Prince Richard who was then an undergraduate. The Princess also attended a language school in London and in 1971 became a secretary at the Royal Danish Embassy. Birgitte left that post shortly before her marriage.

The wedding of Prince and Princess Richard of Gloucester took place on Saturday 8th July 1972. It was no bigger than any that might take place anywhere in Britain, and was, by royal standards, almost humble. The attendance of members of the Royal Family was also minimal. Chief guests were Queen Elizabeth the Queen Mother, The Prince of Wales, The Princess Margaret and the Earl of Snowdon and Princess Alice, Countess of Athlone. The Queen, the Duke of Edinburgh and Princess Anne were on holiday in Scotland, the Duke and Duchess of Kent were at the tennis championships at Wimbledon, and Princess Alexandra, who had an official engagement earlier that day, flew on to Northamptonshire to attend the wedding reception.

Naturally the bridegroom's mother, the Duchess of Gloucester, was present, and there too in his capacity as Best Man was Prince William. Due to ill-health the Duke of Gloucester, who had been bed-ridden for several years, was unable to attend the ceremony but did attend the reception.

Unlike other royal weddings, this particular event was celebrated not in London, but at St Andrew's Church in the hamlet of Barnwell in Northamptonshire which has been the family home of the Gloucesters for some time.

For her marriage, the bride wore a very simple wedding gown designed by Norman Hartnell. Worked with a flower motif and

made of white swiss voile, the gown followed a simple princess line, with high neck, long sleeves, fitted bodice, and long semi-full skirt. The net veil, edged with white piping, reminiscent of Princess Margaret's bridal veil twelve years before, was secured by a band of white flowers, complementing the traditional Danish sheaf she carried as a bouquet. There were no bridal attendants.

Approximately 90 guests heard the Dean of Windsor, assisted by the Bishop of Peterborough and the Rev Peter Bustin, Vicar of Barnwell, marry the couple. The music chosen for the ceremony was 'Easter Song', 'All creatures of our God and King', with music by William Henry Draper, and 'Love Divine all Loves Excelling'.

The crowds turned out, albeit on a smaller scale than those who attend a London Royal Wedding, to see the Royal Family and their guests arrive and to cheer the bride and bridegroom who, due to the steadily falling rain, sheltered beneath a large umbrella as they left the small church. It had been hoped that the Prince and Princess would be able to walk back to Barnwell Manor across a narrow track in the grounds of the house, but they unfortunately needed to use one of the royal cars for the return journey.

For the royal couple, the first two years of their married life were to bring three important occurrences. The Prince became heir to his father in August 1972 on the death of Prince William, and twenty two months later succeeded to the Dukedom of Gloucester. Richard, a prince for thirty years and Birgitte, a princess for less than two years, were now the new Duke and Duchess of Gloucester, and the young Duchess was by this time expecting their first child.

Alexander, Earl of Ulster, was born two months premature in October 1974 and there was at first some concern over the child's condition. However, the couple were delighted with their son who was growing stronger, and in December Lord Ulster was taken home to his parents at Kensington Palace from St Mary's Hospital, Paddington.

ve: Prince Richard of Gloucester with his fiancée Miss Birgitte Van
rs photographed among the flowers of Kensington Palace gardens.
(*Photograph:* Tom Hustler, Camera Press)

Left: Instead of walking back to Barnwell Manor, as planned, the wet weather meant that the couple had to be driven.

(*Photograph:* Fox Phot[o])

Below Left: The rain did not deter the crow[d] from gathering outside St Andrew's Church, Barnwell, for a glimpse of the couple and their guests. (*Photograph:* Fox Phot[o])

Below: The bride photographed at the door [of] Barnwell Manor before leaving for the chur[ch].

(*Photograph:* Tom Hustler, Camera Pre[ss])

Right: Prince William of Gloucester, elder brother of the groom, checks the time as Queen Elizabeth the Queen Mother looks o[n].

(*Photograph:* Tom Hustler, Camera Pre[ss])

Right: The smiling and happy couple cut the cake at their wedding reception. (*Photograph:* Tom Hustler, Camera Pr...

Below Left: Prince Richard protects his bride from the rain as they walk from the church to the waiting cars after the marriage ceremony. (*Photograph:* Fox Photos)

Below: The Queen Mother walks from the church with the bride's father, Mr A P Henriksen. Prince Charles opens his umbrella behind them. (*Photograph:* Fox Phot...

*: Princess Alice, Countess of Athlone,
·ys a joke with Admiral Sir Geoffrey
·wkins at the wedding reception.
(*Photograph:* Tom Hustler, Camera Press)

t: The bride with her mother Mrs
·x-Nielsen, at the reception.
(*Photograph:* Tom Hustler, Camera Press)

·w: The bride and groom smile at each
·r as they leave Barnwell Church.
(*Photograph:* Keystone Press Agency)

Below: The bride and groom with some of their guests.
Seated (left to right) Princess Alice, Countess of Athlone,
the Duchess of Gloucester, the Queen Mother and Mrs Marx-Nielsen,
the bride's mother.
Standing (left to right) Prince Michael of Kent, Princess Margaret,
Prince Charles, the groom, the bride, Prince William of Gloucester,
Miss Susan Van Deurs Henriksen, Mrs Allette Just Christiansen,
(the bride's sisters) and her father, Mr A P Henriksen.

(*Photograph:* Tom Hustler, Camera Press)

Right: Prince and Princess Richard prepare to leave the reception at
Barnwell Manor at the start of their honeymoon.

(*Photograph:* Tom Hustler, Camera Pr

~ANNE AND MARK~

29th May 1973

COURT CIRCULAR

BUCKINGHAM PALACE

IT IS WITH THE GREATEST PLEASURE THAT THE QUEEN AND THE DUKE OF EDINBURGH ANNOUNCE THE BETROTHAL OF THEIR BELOVED DAUGHTER THE PRINCESS ANNE TO LIEUTENANT MARK PHILLIPS, THE QUEEN'S DRAGOON GUARDS, SON OF MR AND MRS PETER PHILLIPS.

So at last the reports that swamped the national newspapers were confirmed in one brief communique issued from Buckingham Palace, despite weeks of denials including quite adamant 'there's nothing to it' rebuffs from the Princess and Lieutenant Phillips.

It was through their mutual love of horses and show jumping that Anne and Mark Phillips first met. Their first meeting was at an equestrian reception in 1968 for the Olympic team and since that time the Princess and Lieutenant Phillips met often at such functions.

As the Royal engagement was making headline news in the press, the Princess and her fiancé, with The Queen, The Duke of Edinburgh, Prince Andrew and Prince Edward were aboard the Royal Train travelling overnight from Aberdeen to London at the conclusion of the Royal Family's annual Highland holiday. The maroon and gold train arrived at King's Cross Station to the cheers and calls of good luck from a crowd of some two thousand people.

The Princess, wearing a blue and white check suit, with her hair pulled back in what the press called 'Tom Jones' style, waved and smiled in response to the enthusiastic cheering which greeted her as she alighted from the train. The Royal party then drove to Buckingham Palace where after lunch they met representatives of the world's press. Mr and Mrs Peter Phillips, Mark's parents, had been invited to lunch at the palace, and when the Royal party came onto the lawns for photographs, they were included in the group.

The Princess and her fiancé became the first royal couple to give an impromptu interview on such an occasion. They both agreed that their feelings for one another had become serious after Badminton. They had actually become engaged at Easter.

An announcement was released shortly afterwards that the wedding of the Princess Anne and Lieutenant Mark Phillips would take place on the morning of Wednesday 14th November 1973 at Westminster Abbey.

Princess Anne, a straightforward young woman, had decided that she wanted her wedding to be as simple as possible. So, while leading fashion houses waited with bated breath for a summons from Buckingham Palace to make the royal wedding gown, Princess Anne casually dropped the bomb-shell to a dumbfounded Maureen Baker of Susan Small Limited, who had made clothes for the Princess for five years. Mrs Baker told the press that she had no idea the Princess would ask her to make the gown. 'I thought I might be asked to contribute towards the trousseau, but felt sure the dress would go to Hartnell or somebody.' As it was, Maureen Baker, who also designs for Princess Alexandra, was responsible for both wedding gown and trousseau.

It was obvious that Princess Anne was going to break with tradition. The choice of designer being her first break, her second was to come when it was announced that there would be only two attendants: one bridesmaid, her 9 year old cousin, Lady Sarah Armstrong-Jones, daughter of Princess Margaret and Lord Snowdon, and one page-boy, her younger brother Prince Edward, also 9 years old.

Generally speaking, royal brides are attended by a minimum of six bridesmaids. In a television interview, screened two days before their marriage, Princess Anne was asked why she had chosen only two attendants. She replied, 'Having been a bridesmaid once or twice myself, I know what it was like having yards of uncontrollable children.'

Some days before the wedding of the Princess to the newly promoted Captain Phillips, the Union Jacks were flying from the white painted flag poles along the Mall, and in front of Buckingham Palace, as the road widens in two half circles, flag poles were erected which were to be draped with specially made banners, on which were set the couple's linked initials 'A' and 'M'.

By Tuesday 13th November all was prepared at Westminster Abbey. The Abbey itself had been closed to the public for nine days prior to the wedding so that all could be arranged within. Special stands were erected, both outside and inside, to accommodate the two hundred journalists from home and abroad assigned to cover

every aspect of the wedding. An estimated audience of 530 millions would watch the wedding, 230 millions more than had watched the wedding of Princess Margaret thirteen years before. The wedding was transmitted to the largest television audience in the history of Royal weddings, as far as the United States of America and Japan, and throughout Europe. It was the first Royal wedding to be shown in colour, and cameras were mounted not only along the processional route but also outside Buckingham Palace, where a stand had been erected on the Victoria Memorial. Inside the Quadrangle of the palace, cameras were set up to record the arrival of the royal bride and her new husband after their marriage.

A section of film showing the bridal pair with their attendants and parents was specially recorded in the Chinese Room beyond the palace balcony. This was incorporated in Her Majesty's Christmas 1973 broadcast to the Nation and Commonwealth countries.

On 13th November, the Princess and Mark attended the final rehearsal of their wedding, along with the Queen, Princess Margaret and various members of the Royal Family.

To avoid disrupting early morning traffic, the carriages had been driven to and from Westminster Abbey in a series of before dawn trial runs so that on the day the timing would be perfect.

The evening of 13th November and the small hours of Wednesday 14th were cold and windy, but even the threat of rain did nothing to deter the thousands of people who flocked to London for the wedding. All along the processional route, people came to snap up the vantage points. Young and old alike arrived on the Mall to sleep under make-shift tents and in sleeping bags. Newspaper vendors sold their early morning copies of the wedding papers. Some carried sketches of the outfits to be worn by the Royal Ladies, and *The Daily Express* carried a sketch of Mark Phillips in his full dress uniform. There was not a hint, however, of the bridal gown. That was under an embargo until the moment the Princess left Buckingham Palace on her way to her wedding.

Shortly before 10.00 am, a contingent of Gurkhas marched down the Mall, and the crowds were now well and truly in position, five and six deep in places. The balcony of Buckingham Palace was draped in red and gold and the State Standard flew from the mast-head. The press took their allotted places on their stand on the Victoria Memorial and the scene was now set for the arrival of the troops.

When they were in position it was time for the guests to arrive. They included British politicians, High Commissioners, Ambassadors and representatives of many countries, friends, and a handful of celebrities from the world of show business and show-jumping.

The Bridegroom's family arrived, taking their places on the left hand side of the High Altar opposite the places to be occupied by the Royal Family.

Royal guests were the next to arrive. Among them were the Crown Prince of Norway with his wife, Crown Princess Sonja, elegant in a turquoise blue silk coat and matching hat; the exiled King and Queen of the Hellenes; the Crown Princess Beatrix of the Netherlands and her husband Prince Claus; the King-designate of Spain, Don Juan Carlos and his wife, the former Princess Sophia of the Hellenes; Prince Rainier and Princess Grace of Monaco, the latter making a delightful picture in a loose fitting white coat and white mink beret style hat, her hands tucked away in a matching white mink muff. There came also a smattering of princes and princesses from now extinct royal houses, such as the Hohenlohe-Langenburgs, relatives of the Duke of Edinburgh. As a final touch before the arrival of the Royal family and the bride, the royal blue carpet stretching the length of the central aisle was given a last sweeping, in full view of the congregation and television viewers.

Outside, The Queen's procession had left Buckingham Palace and was en route to the Abbey. The time was just after 11.00 am. All along the route the excited crowds cheered and waved flags as the royal procession wound its way towards the Abbey.

It had become a most beautiful day, and the breastplates and helmets of the Sovereign's Escort of the Household Cavalry shone like a thousand mirrors. Following two top-hatted, scarlet coated outriders on grey horses was the Scottish State Coach containing The Queen, Queen Elizabeth the Queen Mother and the Prince of Wales with his younger brother, Prince Andrew. The Irish State Coach behind contained Princess Margaret and the Earl of Snowdon. Queen Alexandra's State Coach carried the Duchess of Gloucester with her son, Prince Richard, his wife Birgitte and Prince Michael of Kent. Then followed three state landaus, their hoods pulled up to protect their occupants from the cold. In the first landau sat the Duke and Duchess of Kent with their two eldest children, the Earl of St Andrews and the Lady Helen Windsor. The second landau carried Princess Alexandra, the Hon Angus Ogilvy and their two children, Master James Ogilvy and Miss Marina Ogilvy. The third landau contained The Queen's Mistress of the Robes, the Duchess of Grafton, the Mistress of the Robes to Queen Elizabeth the Queen Mother, the Duchess of Abercorn, the Master of the Horse, the Duke of Beaufort and the Private Secretary to The Queen.

The only procession now to pass by was that of Her Royal Highness The Bride. Precisely at 11.12 am, the bridal carriage passed through the central arch of Buckingham Palace to the strains of 'God Save The Queen' barely audible above the tremendous cheering and applause and the clattering of the horses' hooves.

The Bride's procession was composed of three carriages. First came the Glass Coach; then a state landau in which rode the two small bridal attendants with Miss Mary Dawnay, Lady in Waiting to Her Royal Highness; and finally in another state landau drove Miss Rowena Brassey, Lady in Waiting, and Prince Philip's Private Secretary, Commander William Willett. As Princess Anne drove on her way to the Abbey between the rows of cheering onlookers, The Queen and members of the Royal Family were walking in procession down the aisle of Westminster Abbey. Her Majesty, dressed in a coat of sapphire blue silk and wool, with a matching scarf style hat trimmed with sapphire blue lace, walked beside Queen Elizabeth the Queen Mother, in a coat of pale beige banded with gold lamé and sable and a hat also of sable and gold lamé. Their Majesties were preceded by the remaining members of the Royal Family. The ladies were dressed in an array of autumn colours: Princess Margaret in a coat of brown and gold trimmed with dark sable, with matching turban style hat by Dior of London; The Duchess of Kent, chic and attractive in a velvet coat of amber and ocre shading with a wide brimmed hat to match by Belville Sassoon; Princess Alexandra in a coat and hat of sea green velvet; and the Duchess of Gloucester in an outfit of pale aquamarine.

Following the Queen and The Queen Mother were the Prince of Wales in naval uniform with sword, and Prince Andrew in a plain grey lounge suit.

All was now set for the arrival of the Bride. Her procession drove around Parliament Square past St Margaret's Church to the West Door of Westminster Abbey. Princess Anne alighted, stepping down onto the blue carpet, while Maureen Baker unfolded the bride's train and set it straight. At last the wedding gown was seen in all its magnificence. The commentators and fashion correspondents were ecstatic. 'This beautiful gown', one commentator repeated several times before remembering to describe it.

Slowly, the Bride walked under the awning, hands clasped before her. At the West Door she was handed an attractive shower style bouquet composed of fifteen white roses from Holland, lily-of-the-valley, stems of Dendrobium orchids from Singapore, and stephanotis. The only foliage was lily-of-the-valley leaves, apart from a memento of myrtle, grown in Cowes on the Isle of Wight from a sprig in Queen Victoria's wedding bouquet.

The wedding gown took away the breath of those who saw it, as the bride stood beside her father, obviously not at all nervous and smiling broadly as she talked and joked with the Duke of Edinburgh. It was simple in design, yet surely one of the most original of all modern Royal wedding gowns. The dress followed the traditional Princess line, emphasised with fine graduated pin tucks. The fabric was pure white silk, specially woven for Princess Anne to her designer's requirements. The sleeves were inspired by early Tudor gowns, and they fell to a point just below the Princess's knees. They were set over finely pleated white silk chiffon undersleeves and were edged with pearls and mirror jewels. From the shoulders fell a delicate transparent train made of pure silk net delicately embroidered with floral sprays of silk and silver thread and embellished with pearls and mirror jewels.

Princess Anne's hair, styled by Michael of Michael-John, was parted in the centre, very full on either side and swept up with a hair piece on top. A diamond tiara, loaned by Queen Elizabeth the Queen Mother to her granddaughter, as indeed she had loaned it to The Queen on her wedding day, held in place the full length veil of very fine silk. Behind the Bride stood her two small attendants, Prince Edward in a kilt of Royal Stuart Tartan, with a black velvet jacket and white lace jabot, and Lady Sarah Armstrong-Jones wearing a pinafore dress in pure silk organza, mounted on silk and wool. The lattice-worked sleeves and yoke were in silk organza and satin ribbon, embroidered with 5000 small pearls. This was worn with a matching embroidered Juliet cap.

The flourish of trumpets had sounded the Bride's arrival, and the organ began to play the processional hymn 'Glorious things of thee are spoken'.

The procession began to make its way down the central aisle. The Princess followed the procession of the clergy towards her fiancé, who stood at the foot of the altar steps with his Groomsman, Captain Eric Grounds, both looking splendid in their full dress uniforms. Very slowly the procession moved along the aisle, under the spotlights and the arc-lamps and the series of Waterford Crystal chandeliers given to the Abbey by the Guinness family in the 1960s.

As the Bride approached the altar steps, past the foreign royal guests, Captain Phillips turned his head and gave a brief and somewhat nervous smile. Once she was at his side, Princess Anne turned and handed her bouquet to her bridesmaid. The Dean stepped forward.

'Dearly beloved, we are gathered here in the sight of God and in the face of this congregation to join this man and this woman in Holy Matrimony. . . .' The eagerly awaited marriage of The Princess Anne and Captain Mark Phillips had begun.

The Archbishop of Canterbury in his cope and embroidered

mitre stepped forward to marry the couple. Both the Bride and her Bridegroom's responses were heard loud and clear. The Archbishop pronounced that they be man and wife and raised his hand in blessing . . . God the Father, God the Son, God the Holy Ghost, Bless, preserve and keep you . . .

The Princess, now wearing a wedding ring of plain gold, and her husband moved to the altar. The Abbey choir sang the 23rd Psalm, 'The Lord's my Shepherd', followed by the chant leading into the Lord's Prayer, said by the Precentor of the Abbey with the choir. After a final prayer intoned by the Dean of Westminster and the 'Amen' by Orlando Gibbons, a fanfare was sounded and the National Anthem sung. Then the Bride and Bridegroom and immediate members of their respective families left their places to enter the Chapel of St Edward the Confessor where the Marriage Register was signed. During the signing of the Register the anthem by Ralph Vaughan Williams 'Let all the world in every corner sing' was performed. Another fanfare was sounded and 'Orb and Sceptre' was then played. Princess Anne and her husband appeared in the chapel doorway and as the processional music rang out they moved very slowly forward, Prince Edward straightening his sister's train. The couple turned slightly as they approached The Queen. Princess Anne made a deep curtsey to her mother, and Captain Phillips bowed.

The bridal procession was joined by the Groomsman, and the five walked back down the aisle to Widor's Toccata in F. The Princess chatted to her husband, obviously to calm his nerves.

Outside, the bells of the Abbey were ringing. The bridal pair walked past the soldiers and the Glass Coach moved forward to take them back to Buckingham Palace and the wedding breakfast. The Royal Family, led by The Queen and Prince Philip, with Queen Elizabeth the Queen Mother, stood back as the newly-weds stepped into the Glass Coach, and television viewers saw the Queen, obviously extremely happy and proud, bob up and down on her heels as the carriage pulled away to the deafening cheers of the crowds.

Once back at Buckingham Palace, the Royal Family and their guests sat down to a sumptuous wedding breakfast. The white and silver wedding cake, five tiers high and nearly six feet tall, stood on a sideboard. It had been made by the Army Catering Corps at Aldershot. Later the Princess Anne, who now uses the title Her Royal Highness The Princess Anne, Mrs Mark Phillips, and her husband cut the cake, using Mark's ceremonial sword.

Norman Parkinson, who was responsible for the highly acclaimed 21st birthday photographs of Princess Anne in 1971 and who also took the couple's official engagement photographs, was again commissioned to act as photographer at the wedding. The studies were posed for in the Throne Room at the palace, and apart from Parkinson there were two press photographers who were to take photographs for distribution in the National press the following day.

Shortly after the scheduled time of 1.35 pm, Princess Anne and her husband came out on to the Palace balcony to the tremendous acclaim of the crowds still massed in their thousands beneath. The Queen and Prince Philip, the Prince of Wales and Mark's parents then joined them. Prince Charles, whose 25th birthday it was, won a special cheer and was urged by Anne to make acknowledgement.

The set time for the departure of the couple at the start of their honeymoon was 4.00 pm, and once more the crowds massed on to the Victoria Memorial and into the surrounding roads to catch yet another glimpse of them. Shortly after 4.00 pm, Princess Anne and Captain Mark Phillips emerged from the palace in an open landau, accompanied by an escort of the Household Cavalry, composed of a dozen or so Troopers.

Members of the Royal Family ran after the carriage into the forecourt of Buckingham Palace, throwing confetti and waving their farewells. Princess Anne was wearing another outfit by Susan Small and, as Maureen Baker said, the sapphire blue velvet coat, which was trimmed with a large white mink collar and cuffs, had been matched exactly to the colour of the sapphire in the Princess's engagement ring. John Boyd, the milliner to Her Royal Highness, had created a pill-box style hat in white mink and complete with pom-pom. As the procession, the smallest of the day, moved along Buckingham Palace Road, office workers came on to balconies and out into the street to join the number of well-wishers already there. The couple travelled to the Royal Hospital in Chelsea where one of the Queen's Rolls-Royce cars was waiting to speed them to the privacy of the home of Princess Alexandra and her family, Thatched House Lodge in Richmond Park. Once there, they dined together and watched their wedding on television, just as millions had done earlier.

The following morning, Anne and Mark left Thatched House Lodge for Heathrow Airport to fly out to join the Royal Yacht *Britannia* for their Caribbean honeymoon. They then went immediately on an official visit to Equador, Colombia, Jamaica and Antigua. They returned to England on 17th December.

ove: The two families meet on the lawns of
ckingham Palace. (Left to right) Prince
ilip, Lt Mark Phillips, Princess Anne, Mrs
ne Phillips, HM The Queen and Mr Peter
illips.   (*Photograph:* Fox Photos)

ght: The Princess and her fiancé on their
y to Westminster Abbey for a pre-wedding
nily rehearsal.   (*Photograph:* Fox Photos)

Right: Princess Anne arrives at Westminster Abbey with her father, Prince Philip.
(*Photograph:* Fox Photos)

Below: The Princess smiles to the crowds as the Glass Coach carries her to the Abbey for her wedding. (*Photograph:* Fox Photos)

Left: The Bride's mother and grandmother arrive for the ceremony.

(*Photograph:* Fox Photos)

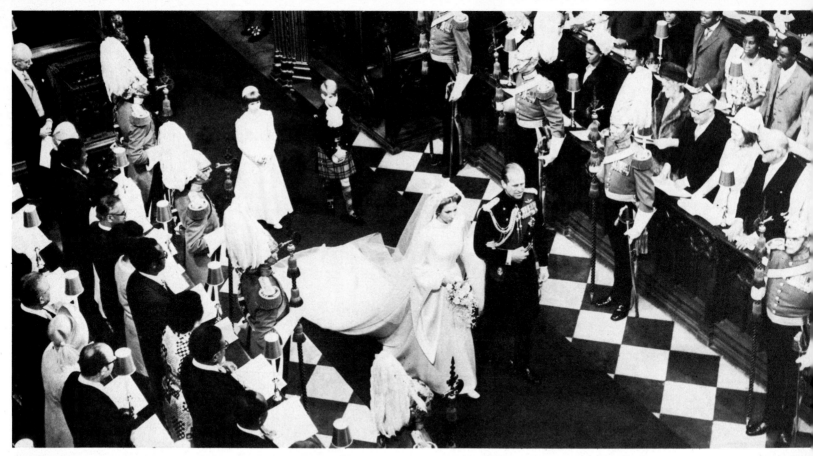

Above: Princess Anne walks up the aisle of the Abbey on the arm of her father, followed by her two attendants, Lady Sarah Armstrong-Jones and Prince Edward.
(*Photograph: Keystone Press Agency*)

Below Far Left: The Princess turns to her waiting attendant before handing over her bouquet. (*Photograph: Fox Photos*)

Below Left: The bride and groom kneel before the altar. (*Photograph: Fox Photos*)

Right: Capt Phillips and Princess Anne leave the vestry after the signing of the register.
(*Photograph: Fox Photos*)

Below: The Archbishop of Canterbury pronounces the blessing over the young couple.
(*Photograph: Fox Photos*)

*: Mr and Mrs Peter Phillips and their
ghter Sarah in Westminster Abbey.
(*Photograph:* Fox Photos)

w Left: Hymn singing during the
mony. (Left to right) The Queen Mother,
ace Philip, and HM The Queen. Behind
n are Prince Michael of Kent and the
chess of Kent. (*Photograph:* Fox Photos)

ht: Capt Phillips bows and Princess Anne
efully curtseys to the Queen while Prince
ard arranges his sister's train.
(*Photograph:* Keystone Press Agency)

w: The smiling bride and groom walk
the Royal Family on their way out of
Abbey. (*Photograph:* Fox Photos)

Left: The Princess and her husband about [to] leave Westminster Abbey after the service. (*Photograph:* Fox Pho[tos])

Below: Princess Anne hands her bouquet to Lady Sarah Armstrong-Jones before getting into her coach. (*Photograph:* Fox Pho[tos])

t: The bride and groom leave their carriage on their arrival at kingham Palace.   (*Photograph:* Fox Photos)

v: An obviously happy Queen leaves the Abbey with her husband, ce Philip.   (*Photograph:* Fox Photos)

Below: A happy group photograph taken at Buckingham Palace during the wedding reception.

Back row: Princess Alexandra and the Hon Angus Ogilvy
Next row: Miss Sarah Phillips, Mr and Mrs Peter Phillips, the Duchess of Kent, Capt Eric Grounds, the best man, Prince Philip, the Duke and Duchess of Gloucester, the Duke of Kent, Prince Charles, Lord Mountbatten
Next row: King Constantine of Greece, Prince Claus, Queen Anne-Marie, the Prince and Princess of Norway, the groom, the b[ride,] HM The Queen, Princess Alice of Gloucester, the Queen Mother, Prince Andrew
Front row, left: Princess Beatrix, Princess Alice, Master James Ogilvy, Prince Edward, Lady Sarah Armstrong-Jones
Right: Princess Margaret, Lord Snowdon, Prince Michael of Kent a[nd] in front of them, Miss Marina Ogilvy, Lord Linley, Lady Helen Windsor and the Earl of St Andrews.   (*Photograph:* Fox Pho[to)]

w: An excited Viscount Linley points out
bride to his parents, Princess Margaret and
d Snowdon, after the wedding.

          (*Photograph:* Fox Photos)

it: Prince Edward, Capt Phillips and
cess Anne wave to the crowds from the
ony of Buckingham Palace.

          (*Photograph:* Keystone Press Agency)

re Right: The bride and groom, looking
oy and relaxed, leave the Palace at the
of their honeymoon.

          (*Photograph:* Fox Photos)

v Right: The Princess and her husband
d the aircraft which is to take them to
West Indies for their honeymoon.

          (*Photograph:* Fox Photos)

ACKNOWLEDGEMENTS

For their generous help in the compilation of THE ROYAL BRIDES I should like to offer my special thanks to:

Her Majesty The Queen for graciously allowing me to reproduce part of a letter written to her by the late King George VI;

Macmillan & Co Publishers, for their permission to reproduce the extract from Sir John Wheeler Bennett's book *King George VI: His Life and Reign;*

Mrs Maureen Baker of Susan Small Limited; Mr John Cavanagh.

For checking facts, my sincere thanks to:

The Press Office of H M The Queen, Buckingham Palace;

The Office of T R H The Duke & Duchess of Gloucester;

The Office of T R H The Duke and Duchess of Kent;

The Office of H R H Princess Alexandra, the Hon Mrs Angus Ogilvy;

The Office of The Dean of Westminster, Westminster Abbey;

The Office of Mr Norman Hartnell, PA, MBE;

Major R A G Courage, MBE;

The Library of *The Daily Express;*

Picture Library, BBC Publications;

Messrs Ron Mulvaney & Bill Hulme, Picture Library, Fox Photos Ltd;

The Picture Library of The Keystone Press Agency Limited. The Picture Library of Camera Press Ltd.

For their unfailing help and encouragement in so many ways I should also like to extend special thanks to the following:

Brian Auld, Maurice Barton, Sara Paul, Nadia Baker, James Sharkey, Max McCann, Maureen Vincent and a host of friends too numerous to list.